TEXAS

Photography by DAVID MUENCH

TEXAS

Text by JERRY FLEMMONS

RAND McNALLY & COMPANY
CHICAGO · NEW YORK · SAN FRANCISCO

Map of TEXAS

Distance scale

0 20 40 60 80 100 120 Miles

0   40   80   120   160 Kilometers

© 1980 Rand McNally & Co.

PHOTO CREDITS

Cletis Reaves, Freelance Photographers Guild, pp. 30–31;
NASA, p. 32 top; Larry Dale Gordon, p. 32 bottom; Jack
Lewis, *Texas Highways*, pp. 66, 70 bottom, 71; Bill Ellzey,
Van Cleve Photography, p. 70 top; H. Armstrong Roberts,
pp. 75, 77; Doris DeWitt, Van Cleve Photography, p. 91.
All other photographs by David Muench.

First printing, 1980

Page One– YUCCAS IN GRASSLAND, MULESHOE NATIONAL WILDLIFE REFUGE
Overleaf– AGAVE PLANT AT THE WINDOW, BIG BEND NATIONAL PARK

Library of Congress Cataloging in Publication Data:

Muench, David.
  Texas.

  1. Texas—Description and travel—1951-
I. Flemmons, Jerry.   II. Title.
F391.2.M83   779'.99764   80-16356
ISBN 0-528-81105-3

Contents

GAILLARDIA DAISIES AND BUTTERCUPS

Introduction

WHEN SPEAKING OF TEXAS IT IS BEST TO BEGIN WITH THE FACT THAT IT IS A SOVEREIGN NATION REDUCED TO STATEHOOD. FOR A DECADE TEXAS MAINTAINED ITS OWN GOVERNMENT, ITS OWN FLAG, army and navy, ambassadorial cadre, foreign treaties, and other requisite paraphernalia of an independent nation. Politically, we were equal to the United States of America as it existed early in the last century.

Texas was drawn into the Union in 1845 for a variety of reasons, most of them financial—the young Republic of Texas badly mismanaged its meager treasury. But the United States needed Texas because of its strategic location in relation to Mexico and its position astride the path of western expansion. It was a seller's market, and we joined America under conditions that suggest a corporate merger rather than a mere induction into statehood, for several Constitutional authorities argue that Texas retained the right to withdraw from its confederation with the United States at any time it chose.

Sam Houston, Texas's great political mystic and first president, once said, "Texas could exist without the United States but could the United States, except at very great hazard, exist without Texas?" An interesting question, and one that has spawned a game we Texans play now and then, mostly for our own amusement, but also to demonstrate what America would lack without us.

The numbers change from time to time, but it is generally conceded that Texas of the 1980s—should it choose to withdraw from the Union and once again become independent—would rank among the world's wealthiest nations, with a per capita income on a par with that of Sweden, West Germany, and the United States, though somewhat behind that of Kuwait.

It would be the fifth largest petroleum-producing nation on earth. It would be fifth in cotton production, twelfth in numbers of beef cattle, sixth in numbers of television stations, fourteenth in beer brewing, and eighth in automobile registrations (well ahead of Russia).

Should Texas secede, it would begin its new nationhood with most of the shiny doodads of modern progressive countries, including its own space hardware and space exploration program (out of NASA's Houston headquarters) and the H-bomb—yes, Texas makes hydrogen bombs at a Pantex Corporation plant near Amarillo in the upper Panhandle.

With the Lone Star missing from the American flag, the United States economy would suffer. Texas produces more than one-third of America's petroleum products and almost 50 percent of its cotton. It is the country's largest producer of beef and of grain sorghums, the second largest electronics manufacturer, and the biggest supplier of computer software. But, lamentedly, it is only the fifteenth-ranked grower of hogs.

The forested lands of East Texas encompass more area than New England. Texas's Brewster County is larger than Connecticut, and Big Bend National Park is greater in size than Rhode Island.

As a sovereign nation, Texas would have 367 miles of coastline on the Gulf of Mexico and four major deepwater ports, 90 mountains more than a mile high, 6,000 square miles of lakes and rivers (more surface water than any other state).

Three cities would rank in size among America's top ten—Houston, Dallas, and San Antonio. There would be a dozen top professional sports teams, 300 important museums, 28 symphony orchestras, six opera companies, 37 corps de ballet, more than 100 state parks and recreation areas, a dozen national parks, seashores, historical monuments, and the like.

Texas would have one of North America's longest rivers (the Rio Grande) and its shortest (the Comal), three-quarters of all the different bird species found in America, 142 species of animals, 100 species of snakes (including 16 poisonous varieties).

In this newly independent nation of Texas, there would be more miles of paved roads and streets and railroad tracks, and more airports, horses, and pickup trucks than in any state and most geographical regions of the United States.

All of this coup-counting chauvinism appears preposterously silly, except that in 1915 there was a serious move in the Panhandle to secede and become "The State of Jefferson." That was entirely legal under another curious provision of Texas's statehood agreement with the United States. At its option, Texas may divide itself into as many as five parts (two more than all of Gaul, waggish historians enjoy pointing out).

No serious division plans have been advanced since the late 1930s, when a portion of East Texas wanted to break away. Legislators defeated that proposal 33 to 15. An earlier plan, advocated before 1900, split Texas in half and suggested that the Panhandle be sold to the United States as an Indian reservation.

Serious students of the five-out-of-one statehood plan argue that Texas would increase its senatorial representation in Washington by eight if the state were divided. But realists suggest that very soon the new senators would be fighting among themselves, and for their respective states. This position does not lack validity, since from the beginning of statehood some stalwarts have assumed that Texas would split up and, as *Texas Monthly* magazine has said, "The surprise is that Texas is still together at all."

That lengthy catalog of Texas superlatives—Texas's "Pandemic of Adjectivitis," someone once called it—is precisely why outsiders view Texans as boasters and braggarts. Our answer is, Truth is Truth and Facts are Facts, but we are hardly modest about it or them.

We Texans are a braggy, theatrical bunch and always have been. We bear the burden of a rich land made infinitely richer by the endless legends and myths we eternally perpetuate, enlarge, and glorify, the lexicon born in and arising from the cult of the cowboy.

It is all illusionary today—the fantasy of cowboyism, the western Yippee Syndrome of spurs that jingle, jangle, jingle, of hats as large as Bangalore parasols, of boots smeared with the residue of cowlots, of the shoot-'em-up *cum* cattle imagery evoked by uttering that historic, heroic, metaphorical, blessed name. Texas.

Texas. A frazzled and brittle truth, well-worn but worn well, like an old favorite jacket too comfortable to be discarded.

I no longer know a single real cowboy, but I am acquainted with one Texan who owns diamond-studded boots, another who plays golf in his alligator boots, and another, a lawyer, whose cowboy boots are handmade in Italy. Several men I know own western-cut tuxedoes, worn of course with their "formal" patent leather boots and silver-tipped fancy string ties.

I don't own a cow nor do any of my friends, although someone here must because Texas has more cattle than any other state. More horses, too, although I haven't seen one in years outside rodeos and stock shows and riding stables. They have been chased from the range by Jeeps and other modern ranching equipment.

However fantasized or incongruous, cowboyism is endemic in the Texas of the 1980s. We've outgrown cowboyism, but we refuse to banish it forever to the pulp pages and silver screen where it rightfully belongs. We cling to our romanticized notions of Texas, though we long ago ceased to live up to their pretentions, if indeed we ever did.

What truly remains of the myths is the land, principally West Texas, which was the original domain of the cowboy. West Texas dominates the state, in fact and in legend. Fully one-half of Texas has the physiognomy of dry flatness, of horizontal stark majesty, and it is *that* Texas which comes to mind when outsiders think of the state. It matters little that the rest of Texas has a kind of pastoral softness—the pine forests of East Texas, the rolling central hills, the white beaches of the Gulf, and the tropical valley of the south. And it is of no consequence that today more cattle are raised on the sweet grasses of East Texas than in West Texas or that East Texas truly owns the state's oil wealth. To foreigners educated by the legends of cowboys and prairies, Texas *is* West Texas and that's that.

Texas is an immense place, and within it West Texas is a region unto itself. Drive from East Texas, say from Texarkana on the Arkansas border, to El Paso in the farthest corner of West Texas and the highway distance is about 700 miles. From high in the Panhandle of West Texas to deepest South Texas is a distance of 800 miles. In between is an immensity unbelieved by those who don't live here. And half of that great vastness is West Texas, or what people have come to believe is West Texas. The cult of cowboyism and the braggadocio of Texans have forever engraved that image in the minds of people around the world.

Today if you would define Texas, it must be by its appalling size and its insuperable genius for evading any sure definition. What it appears to be, it is not, or seems not to be, although one can never be certain.

"A vast gray sea of vague tedium," a detractor once said of the state. This vastness, the physical immensity of the land, intimidates others, and Texans, a generally unbridled bunch, intimidate outsiders. We intimidate and anger, confound and dismay, and in turn are scorned and praised in about equal portions.

"No one feels neutral about Texas," *Venture* magazine reported long ago. "It is a state that arouses more feeling, pro and con, than any other in the Union."

That's true, and the myths serve to intensify those feelings. The legends just won't go away, because we hold them so dear.

But what may finally erase them are the new Texans who, as the 1980s began, were arriving in greater and greater numbers. As the fancy buckle on the Sunbelt, that warm-weather strip of the southern United States, Texas has become the country's fastest growing state.

For whatever reasons all those outsiders flooded into the state, they found an unexpected Texas, a sophisticated, urban society, where more than half the population now lives in Houston, Dallas/Fort Worth, San Antonio, and El Paso; a fine climate; low prices; available jobs; and friendliness.

They also found the cult of the cowboy, and many immediately adopted its casual jeans-and-boots garb as their own. To the newcomers, cowboyism is something less than it is to native Texans, not worse, but less—and different. Ultimately, they will change it, the impression Texas makes on the rest of the world, though the process will be long and hard.

Speaking of these new Texans, *Texas Monthly* publisher William Broyles said to his readers, "The question of the 1980s is whether they will Americanize us before we Texanize them."

Whatever the answer, change will come to Texas, and to everything Texan—everything, that is, except the immensity of the land. That will never change.

The VALLEY and GULF COAST

THE MYTH OF THE RIO GRANDE IS IN THE BRAVURA OF ITS NAME, AND THE BELIEF THAT IT EXISTS AT ALL. NEITHER GREAT NOR GRAND AS THE SPANISH FOUND AND NAMED IT—PERHAPS BECAUSE THEY CAME UPON THE STREAM from desert wilderness—the river is merely a thin sorrel seam between Texas and Mexico. Wandering and lethargic in Texas, its appearance denies the geographical fact that it is America's second longest river system.

The Rio Grande is born of melting glacial snow 12,-000 feet up in the Colorado Rockies and roves through New Mexico, arriving in Texas at El Paso to become a serpentine 1,248-mile-long international border. Reality is that the Rio Grande scarcely exists as its channel reaches Texas. Its water has been waylaid, impounded and siphoned off for irrigation back there in New Mexico, and through El Paso the stream is little more than an often dry concrete canal.

Were it not for the Conchos River from Mexico, a major tributary entering below El Paso at Presidio, and later the brackish waters of the Pecos River, the Rio Grande perhaps could not live at all.

With the water from the Conchos, the Rio Grande again becomes a coursing river, however unattractive its appearance. Only within the Big Bend, that austere wilderness protruding from the southwest body of Texas, does the stream demonstrate spirit. In the Big Bend, through its spectacular rock-walled canyons, the river splashes and rushes and then, its forced tantrums abated, settles once again into a winding path toward the Gulf of Mexico.

Often narrow and muddy, in stretches nearly exhausted of water by irrigation needs, the Rio Grande courses southeast across nub-ends of the Chihuahuan Desert, is dammed twice—above Del Rio to form Lake Amistad, and below Laredo to create Falcon Reservoir—before gently reaching the slender shred of tropical Texas.

Although the Rio Grande is essentially unnavigable, it has been artificially widened beyond Brownsville to accept ocean freighters and tankers. Finally it is gone, only a khaki-colored stain on the sea.

The Rio Grande, then, has no dramatic overall setting or surge, no imperious character to explain its American name, nor even the Mexican designation, Rio Bravo. It simply is a diplomatic comma between Texas and Mexico, a handy administrative device separating political entities. The frailty of this meandering waterway belies its importance in New World history.

The first true explorers of North America, the Spanish conquistadores, crossed the Rio Grande early in the 16th century to examine, to occupy, what would become Texas and the American Southwest. Decades before Englishmen huddled in their ill-constructed log houses in New England, Spanish settlers had established busy villages along the Rio Grande; and while Puritans scratched in the East Coast earth with sharpened sticks, the Spanish and the Indians they had encountered in the Rio Grande Valley were raising fields of vegetables and grains. While some Eastern colonists sought and killed witches to satisfy the curious dictates of their Puritan religion, the Spanish god was being worshipped in thriving missions spread over a thousand miles of Texas and the Southwest.

The Rio Grande has owned many names. Indians called it P'osoge, "River of Great Water." Antonio de Espejo, coming upon the stream in 1582, named it Rio del Norte, and it appeared on early Spanish maps as Rio Ganapetuan and Rio de Buenaventura. Other explorers designated the stream Rio Turbio because of its frantic flooding nature in the spring.

By the time Antonio Lopez de Santa Anna and his armies retreated south of the river in 1836 after their defeat at San Jacinto, it finally had been accepted as Rio Grande del Norte and acknowledged by Mexico to be the southern boundary of a new and sovereign nation, the Republic of Texas.

Another earlier name was Rio de las Palmas, a legacy of Alonso Alvarez de Piñeda, who led an exploratory force to the river's delta in 1519. He and his men found palm forests along its banks, palms that are today the stately sentinels of Texas's Rio Grande Valley.

It is a soft summery place, the Rio Grande Valley, tropical, punctuated with exotic flora, cooled by Gulf breezes. No more than 50 miles wide, the fertile valley is a precise gameboard of geometrically designed vegetable fields and citrus groves, all existing only because the waters of the Rio Grande are diverted for irrigation.

There is a decidedly Latin vibrancy to the Valley. Spanish is heard as often as English. The foods are peppery, the lifestyle animated. Valley Texans have little in common with the laconic Panhandle cowboy and oil field toolpusher from Tulia up there almost 800 miles away. That the Valley's Spanish-speaking lettuce farmer and the twangy wheatgrower of the Panhandle both are Texans is only a matter of geographic circumstance. Otherwise they have no more in common than the bedouin of Tunisia and the shopkeeper in Johannesburg, whose only bond is living in Africa.

Down along the Rio Grande, isolated by distance and insulated by a harsh finger of the Chihuahuan Desert, the Valley Texan is dependent on the sullen whims of his river and the meager water it provides for sustaining life. His counterparts in Northern Mexico are largely captives of the same circumstance, and they cling to the other bank of the river as tenaciously as their Texas neighbors. Those Rio Grande towns facing one another across the river—Brownsville/Matamoros, McAllen/Reynosa, Laredo/Nuevo Laredo, Eagle Pass/Piedras Negras, Del Rio/Ciudad Acuña—are, in reality, communities separated only by the exigency of government. Casually, easily, the peoples of two nations move back and forth across the river, their way of life fashioned and sustained by the graceless, inelegant little stream called the Rio Grande.

There is also this about the Rio Grande Valley: It is the terminus, particularly along the lower Gulf Coast, for North America's migratory bird population. Along with numerous Texans and northerners, especially Canadians, the birds settle in the Valley for winter warmth beside the placid resacas—freshwater marshes—to immerse themselves in the pleasurable Latin vitality of it all.

Winter in the Valley is a textbook theory, an obscure calendar event, and when spring arrives, it is heralded not by the lessening of cold weather but by the annual phenomenon of marching flowers.

Spring comes by the senses. There is a touch to it, a taste and smell, and there is a warm conspiracy. Late within the almanacical winter of South Texas the flowers assemble, muster in bivouac along the Rio Grande's banks, beside the resacas, and then by some inherent command of nature, sweep northward through the state's midsection, foraging on sunshine and sweet rains, urged along by agreeable winds.

Bluebonnets, the state flower, are the advance shock troops. Behind them are battalions of bachelor's buttons and the red sage called Indian fire, camp followers like the blue gilia, yellow buttercups, and *helianthus annus,* the ebony-eyed sunflower.

This northward surge of wild flowers each spring is a stunning experience. You may, if you wish, clock the marching flower army. It parades up the spine of Texas, spreading ever more widely, at the speed of about 15 miles a day.

One morning a grassy field is gray and lifeless, the next it is smeared with colors: the reds, oranges, and yellows of Indian blanket, the dark-trimmed amber of Mexican hat, the whites of wild indigo and cactus blossoms and rain lilies, the azures of bluebells and wild phlox, the purple of verbena.

A bravura of colors sweeping northward with the spring, and with the flowers travel the migratory wild birds and the winter tourists in their trailers, all set into motion by some internal natural clock and the tan waters of the seemingly inconsequential Rio Grande.

The flower stood alone, its roots somehow imbedded in a placket of soil laid in the scar of a giant trunk of mahogany. The tree, perhaps from the Yucatan or Belize or even as far away as South America, had made its voyage across the Gulf of Mexico and pushed up on Padre Island, then was lifted by a storm and hidden amid the dunes of America's great barrier island. Now it lay half-buried in sand and shrouded by sea grapes and salt grasses.

I was at the lower end of the island, north of the Rio Grande's delta, where it disappears into Gulf waters through Brazos Santiago Pass, north of the fishing village of Port Isabel with its ancient lighthouse and net-hung shrimp boats and graying beach cottages.

The flower was a mutant maverick of the bluebonnet, a stalk of rare white blossoms cupped like old women's hooded caps, rising from that alien mahogany corpse. By any reasonable botanic understanding, the pale flower should not be there, could not grow along the beach sprayed with salt, yet there it grew, defiant, ghostly white, and alone.

How did the seed reach that thin hollow of soil? Clinging perhaps to the fur of a coyote, one of hundreds which still wander and scavenge among Padre's dunes? Camped on the beach at night, you can hear them call, their howls melding with the Gulf winds and surf sounds to form an eerie melange. More likely, the seed courier had been a bird, 350 species of which nest around the island, especially in the marshes of Laguna Madre, the narrow lagoon between Padre and South Texas. There are great horned owls and blue herons, the ubiquitous gulls and terns, marsh hawks and sandhill cranes, and in winter residence, thousands of geese and wild ducks.

That aberrant albino bluebonnet and I shared the dunes of Padre. As far as I could see in either direction, the island was deserted.

Padre is the longest barrier island in the world. Its northern tip touches on Corpus Christi, then for 113 miles the island guards the lower Texas coast, ending where the Rio Grande joins the sea near Port Isabel.

This scimitar of white sand is at the most three miles wide, but usually is no more than a few hundred yards of beach and dunes and aloneness. Its 80-mile-long midsection, now designated a national seashore, is prohibited to all but four-wheel-drive vehicles, and then only by permit, thus ever is uncrowded.

He is gone now, but long ago, before Padre was preserved and protected, a beachcomber lived on the island, up near Corpus Christi, and I visited him often. His name was Roderick. He lived in a one-room hut of his own design and creation, a sturdy shack built of whatever the Gulf tossed up on the beach—bamboo thick as porch posts, oily dock pilings from some hurricane-raked port of the Caribbean, cherrywood logs from Central America—just treasure rubbish from the sea, stacked, nailed, and bound by nylon rigging ropes.

Roderick was a gentle man, bearded of course as a proper beachcomber should be, and he made a little money by selling what he salvaged from the white sand. Glass floats, salt-bleached surrealistic-shaped driftwood, shells. The shells of Padre—sand dollars, Scotch bonnets, spiny murex—fascinated Roderick and he kept the prettier ones for himself, storing them in an old icebox that had floated in with the tide.

When I visited Roderick he would show off his shell inventory, carefully offering for inspection the ribbed cockles and pink tellins, the chalk-white whelks, the giant conches. Surely Roderick's icebox shell trove was worth many hundreds of dollars to collectors, yet he spurned offers from dealers. Roderick loved his shells.

He lived in his shack many years and then one morning he was gone, never to be seen again. Perhaps he moved to another beach, though that is unlikely; good beaches like Padre are few. Maybe he went inland for a job, a home, a family. No one knows. He vanished, deserting his precious shells, which were soon scattered among other collectors and even some shell dealers. The rumor was that Roderick had unearthed the golden treasure of Jean Lafitte, the pirate.

Buried treasure is a reality in the history of Padre Island. It is there, somewhere in the dunes. Perhaps Roderick did find a store of it, and today is living in splendor.

Lafitte, legend says, buried a fortune in gold somewhere on Padre, under a flat round millstone in a field of sea oats. Later, after many storms, the treasure's location was changed in appearance by shifting dunes and the pirate could never again find it.

That is the pattern of treasures on Padre Island. John Singer—of the sewing machine Singers—ranched on the

RIO GRANDE BELOW FALCON

Above– CABBAGES ON THE RIO GRANDE PLAIN
Below– YOUNG CORN CROP AND CABBAGE PALMS, RIO GRANDE PLAIN NEAR HARLINGEN

island during the Civil War but fled when Union ships began patrolling offshore. Before leaving, Singer buried gold and silver worth $62,000 in an old stone crock. Four feet down and sitting on two silver bars. A hurricane in the mid-1860s obliterated the site and Singer was unable to find his fortune. Treasure hunters have searched around Singer's Santa Cruz ranch site, but the gold and silver cache has never been found.

Santa Cruz, 25 miles north of Port Isabel, was home to the island's original settler, Father Nicolas Balli. The Spanish padre came to the island, then called Isla Blanca, in about 1800, but his title to the land was withdrawn after the revolution of 1846. By that time, the island was called Padre, after Balli. During the U.S.–Mexican War, General Zachary Taylor's troops used the Santa Cruz ruins as a base camp, and his soldiers, as have thousands of treasure hunters since, searched the island for Spanish gold said to be buried there.

Once there was a dune 15 miles north of Port Isabel called Money Hill where treasure hunters over the years found golden Spanish coins dating from the 1500s. Another hurricane erased Money Hill in 1916 and nothing has been discovered there since.

Perhaps the gold coins came from the wreck of Spanish treasure ships in 1553. Twenty ships left Mexico laden with New World gold for Spain. Near Cuba a hurricane struck the fleet and many galleons were blown westward and wrecked on the shores of Padre Island. About 300 survivors came ashore 20 miles south of what is now Corpus Christi (this much is known to be true; divers have found remains of a Spanish galleon, coins, and other artifacts offshore). Once on the beach, the shipwrecked Spaniards encountered another notorious legend of Padre's dunes—the fierce Karankawa Indians.

Early Spanish and French explorers ascribed to the Karankawas mythical characteristics, including giantism and cannibalism. Seven feet tall, the tribe's warriors were said to be, and armed with persimmon-wood bows no normal man could pull. "Demons from Hell!" Lafitte called the Karankawas and recorded: "They ate two of my men." Texas historian William Edward Seyers described them as "tattooed ghouls reeking with alligator grease, mud, and shark oil." Fray Gaspar Jose de Solis reported to his superior in Spain in 1768 of the island Indians' rites of cannibalism. There is no doubt that they were savage and did engage in some man-eating rituals, but no archeological or anthropological evidence has been found showing that the Karankawas practiced wholesale cannibalism.

The 300 shipwrecked Spaniards immediately were attacked by the Indians and fled south down the island. All but two men were slain by the Karankawas. One survivor was Fray Marcos de Mena, who stumbled into Veracruz with his horrid tale of massacre. The other was Don Francisco Vasquez, who hid in the dunes as the Spanish fled south with the Karankawas close behind. He lived in one of the wrecked galleons until Spanish soldiers came to rescue the treasures strewn on Padre Island.

As the dunes of the island are constantly wiped away by storms, so the Karankawas were wiped away by soldiers, civilization, and time, and the last survivor of the tribe is said to have died late in the last century in northern Mexico, a gentle farmer of quite ordinary stature and appetite.

The Karankawas, like the tales of treasure, belong to the history of Padre Island. Today the island is a national treasure and those who go there do so for the splendor of its isolated beaches, the lure of the Spanish gold, the warmth of the sun, the myriad birdlife.

That early spring when I discovered the white bluebonnet growing in the mahogany log, I remained a long time in the dunes watching a hawk circle overhead, meadowlarks forming nests in the sea grasses, yellow and white butterflies swarming over the sea grapes. Late in the evening a V of Canada geese rose from the marshes of Laguna Madre and flew north, and I followed.

From Beaumont beside the Louisiana border in the north to the Rio Grande in the south, Texas has 367 miles of coastline. Corpus Christi, at the upper tip of Padre Island, is the state's prettiest coastal city, white and clean, built on and below a high bluff beside the Gulf at the mouth of the Nueces River.

The city was founded in 1839 as a trading post and became a center for tanning cattle hides. It remains in the hide tanning business, as evidenced by bikini-clad bodies decorating Padre's beaches. The port of Corpus Christi is the sea outlet for Texas's coastal plains, a stretch of flatness, of oil wells, and cows. At its back door is the King Ranch, the world's largest cattle operation (833,000 acres). Houston is 150 miles northeast, Mexico, 100 miles south.

Gateway to Padre Island, Corpus Christi is connected to the curved sliver of sand by causeway. Weekend sun worshippers roam Nueces County Park, at the north end of Padre. I walked there in late afternoon, frightening the ghost crabs and laughing gulls. There was sun enough and sea breezes, fishermen hip-deep in the water, kids molding sand mountains. Even a few surfers were out, though surfing on Texas's Gulf Coast is much like snowskiing in Iowa, mostly wishful thinking; waves lap, rarely leap, at Padre.

Across a narrow cut is Mustang Island, another barrier curb of sand embracing the outer edge of Corpus Christi Bay. At its northern end is Port Aransas, a fishing village. A ferry—one of only three remaining in Texas—operates between Port Aransas and Aransas Pass, which has become a flourishing art center set amid a stand of coastal oaks. North from Aransas Pass is Rockport, outside of which is the Aransas Wildlife Refuge, wintering ground for that rarest of water fowl—the whooping crane.

Thousands of visitors annually trek through the Aransas Wildlife Refuge to view those leggy, gawky birds. Few more than five dozen whooping cranes remain in the world. Shy as budding social ingenues, the whoopers arrive at the refuge in mid-autumn to stage their flapping, ritualistic breeding dances and nest in the tall grasses. They are difficult to see, even from the high towers or from boats along the Intracoastal Canal, except with powerful binoculars, and many visitors go away without ever viewing the cranes.

Annually, in early spring, the whoopers, adults and the few newborn children, fly away north again to summer near Canada's Great Slave Lake. Awkward, inelegantly graceless on the ground, the whooping crane in flight is a rare and beautiful thing of nature.

The whoopers' flight pattern is north along the Texas coast, leaving the sea near Beaumont, which rests on the cusp of the state's piney woods.

The upper coast is less attractive than the southern shores. Sand there is gray, not white, and beaches are narrower, rockier. It is an important ecological area, however, especially at Sea Rim State Park, a 15,000-acre preserve of marshes in Sabine Pass.

Those salt tidal marshlands create the perfect food chain and nursery for marine life, from shrimp to redfish, and a refuge for animals from mink to the endangered red wolf and alligator.

Midway along the coast is the last of Texas's barrier islands, Galveston, a popular seaside resort and once the principal Gulf entry point for thousands of immigrants arriving for a new life in the American Southwest. Many of those hopeful pioneers came because of the siren call of a pair of brothers from New York who founded what one day would become a megalopolitan phenomenon.

Houston, quite simply, is astonishing. No American city is growing faster. Twenty percent annually. A thousand new citizens each and every week. Four hundred automobiles daily added to the freeway system. New buildings and new businesses.

There is a pulsating vigor and zeal to Houston which, during the decade of the 1970s, denied the recessions and economic sputterings seemingly endemic to the rest of the world.

In 1836 the Republic of Texas was born in a battle against the Mexican army beside what is now the Houston Ship Channel. Almost immediately thereafter a pair

WHITE PELICANS, CORPUS CHRISTI

of New York brothers, Augustus C. and John K. Allen, platted a city, named it for Sam Houston, and began advertising for new citizens—somewhat sheltering the truth about conditions in their locale. What the Allen brothers sold were homesites in a 6,642-acre tract of land (for which, it is said, they paid only $9,428) in the middle of a mosquito-plagued, summer-steaming swamp. Newcomers came, though, and Houston grew. It was the capital of Texas until 1839 when lawmakers, wearied of fighting mosquitoes and fever, transferred their headquarters to Austin in the dry, rolling hills of Central Texas.

No matter, Houston prospered from the beginning to become a bayou Brobdingnagian. Or as O. Henry, that Texas-born short story writer of the last century, characterized it: Baghdad on the Bayou.

And from the beginning, Houston had that innate financial spark. "After you've listened to the talk," it once was said, "you begin to feel that the creation of the world, the arrangement of the solar system, and all subsequent events, including the discovery of America, were provisions of an all-wise Providence, arranged with a direct view to the advancement of the commercial interests of Houston." That was back in 1883 and already Houston was in the business of doing business, was already inventing the future.

"Remember, Bill, Hell and Houston both begin with an h," warned one of those early Allen-enticed settlers to a friend back home. Houston has improved since then, especially with the innovation of air conditioning, which made summers tolerable, and the sudden critical importance of the world's energy needs.

Houston has made itself the financial keystone of the energy industry. It's a push-button city. Pour crude oil and gas in. Push a button. Out flow gasoline and plastics and

CATTLE AND EGRETS, KING RANCH

a thousand other petrochemical products. As headquarters for most of America's major oil companies, Houston is an electric, eclectic city.

It can absorb a thousand newcomers a week since, in the late 1970s, there was almost no unemployment. Two billion dollars' worth of goods—oil field equipment, construction materials, tools, and foodstuffs such as rice —were shipped out of Houston's port annually to Arab countries alone. The Middle East-and-Houston partnership was a natural. That boots-and-burnoose association gave Houston businesses long range contracts with Arab interests amounting to more than $3 billion, when the rest of America and Texas combined had not even approached that astonishing level in Middle East trade.

It is not at all surprising that an Egyptian official once commented, "In the Middle East, the image of an American is that of a big, tall, open-faced Texan who talks loud, has an easygoing manner, a simple sense of humor, and who is grand in his way." Unsaid was the fact that most of those grand Texans were Houstonian.

Houstonian. A regal term, the root of which, I presume, would be *Houstonia.* A city-state, like old Sparta or Athens.

The soaring Free State of Houston, which has regenerated with energy and imagination, is exemplified in its inner city where new brick and steel skyscrapers rise as the center of America's energy future. Growth and expansion occur with almost casual indifference. Texas Transmission Corporation purchased 32 square blocks of downtown Houston, cleared the entire area, and began building anew, a project said to be the largest private urban development in history.

All of this has made Houston into an international city. It is aswarm with Brazilian industrialists, German technocrats, Arab princes in flowing robes.

Between business deals, Houston is a hospitable place, outdoor-oriented, leisurely paced, urbane if somewhat plain-spoken, sophisticated but unsnobbish, polished, if not to a high gloss.

Despite the rising skyline the city is horizontal, not vertical. From Allen's Landing Park, headquarters of those New York-bred brothers, it spreads in a series of concentric concrete freeway circles and other highway spokes to cover an outlandish 600 square miles. Like Los Angeles, Houston is a city of vehicles, where without wheels one is not just reduced to pedestrian status, but is stranded as though set down on the moon, which, by the way, several Houston residents have been.

Except for the summer heat, Houston is a mild-climated city built at the confluence of several geographical and botanical streams, which explains how lawns and parks have pines and palms, oaks and cacti growing side by side. Northward, Houston is touched by East Texas's pine forests and the primeval Big Thicket National Preserve. West are gentle rolling plains and the more typical Texas. Southward is tropical, a land of citrus groves and balmy weather. East—40 miles away—is the Texas Gulf shore, pivoted on Galveston.

Despite a gentle climate that makes Houston a shirt-sleeve town where one may play tennis or golf every day without fear of impending snow blizzards, all major pro-fessional sports are performed indoors, specifically in the Astrodome, a 21st-century widget that is still waiting for the future to arrive.

Not surprisingly, Astroworld USA, a theme park adjacent to the domed stadium, boasts the world's fastest roller coaster, which even on its best day can't keep up with Houston. The city, seemingly ever in the throes of imagination, always is proving itself not just ahead of the pack, but ahead of the pack's vision.

The world-famous Texas Medical Center coordinates health education, medical research, and patient-care facilities on a vast scale. It is not unusual for patients to travel thousands of miles to be treated at this $600 million complex.

The downtown Civic Center, almost surrealistic with its steel and glass structural creations, is an encounter with architectural utopianism, if only because of the chrome-plated fire plug sitting beside the curb. Inside the Center are the Sam Houston Coliseum and Music Hall, the block-sized Jesse H. Jones Hall for the Performing Arts, and the nationally acclaimed Alley Theatre.

Additionally, Houston has a world-class opera company and professional ballet troupe. The Houston Symphony, which long ago played "Old Black Joe" at every concert because that was the favorite tune of the orchestra's most generous financial angel, performs to sell-out audiences. There is modern art in the Contemporary Arts Museum, ancient art in the Museum of Fine Arts, and early Americana at Bayou Bend, former residence of Miss Ima Hogg, daughter of a Texas governor. Visitors also enjoy touring Houston's Zoological Gardens; the San Jacinto Battleground, where Texas won its independence; and the NASA Lyndon B. Johnson Space Center, where NASA engineers and astronauts speak across space and plot for the future of space travel.

Houston is the city with men who have walked on the sands of the moon and the sands of Saharan oil fields, but its phenomenal growth has not been without pain. There are pockets of ugly poverty. Air pollution has reached a critical level. Traffic congestion is a plague. Crime rates are high.

Yet Houston greets the 1980s as America's fifth largest city, reaching toward the fourth position, and owning creditable statistics suggesting that, within this century, it will be the country's largest metropolitan area.

"Houston is totally without the normal rationales of geography and evolutionary social growth that have traditionally created urban centers and culture," wrote urban critic Ada Louise Huxtable. "And yet as a city, a 20th-century city, it works remarkably well. This city bets on a different and brutal kind of distinction—of power, motion, and sheer energy. Its values are material fulfillment, mobility, and mass entertainment. What Houston possesses to an exceptional degree," she declared, "is an extraordinary vitality."

Perhaps Houston already is the city of the future.

A friend of mine calls Houston a petropolis, neither Texan nor American, but of the world, beyond any sure explanation or understanding. Then he offers the perfect definition of the city: "Houston is," he says, "that's all, it just is."

Above– YUCCA AND EBONY, RIO GRANDE DELTA NEAR BROWNSVILLE
Below– LIVE OAK IN BRAZOS LOWLANDS NEAR ANGLETON
Right– SABAL PALMS IN AUDUBON SANCTUARY, RIO GRANDE PLAIN

Left– PRICKLY PEAR CACTUS AND SEASHORE, PADRE ISLAND
Above– SHELLS ON BEACH AT SEA RIM STATE PARK
Below– FOREDUNES ON NORTH PADRE ISLAND

Left– SHRIMP BOAT AGAINST CORPUS CHRISTI SKYLINE
Above– PRESIDIO LA BAHIA WITH BELL TOWER, GOLIAD
Below– BISHOP'S PALACE, GALVESTON
Overleaf– HOUSTON ASTRODOME

Above– NASA'S JOHNSON SPACE CENTER, HOUSTON
Below– SPACE LANDER #2 AT SPACE CENTER
Right– OIL DERRICKS AT SPINDLETOP

Left– SAN JACINTO MONUMENT
Above– RESTORED HOUSE IN SAM HOUSTON PARK, HOUSTON
Below– EAST END OF HOUSTON SKYLINE
Overleaf– CENTRAL HOUSTON SKYSCRAPERS

EASTERN WOODLANDS

I WISH YOU HAD KNOWN LANCE ROSIER. HE WAS A SKINNY-NECKED, SLUMP-SHOULDERED, BRIGHT-EYED RARE OLD MAN WHO NEVER WEIGHED MORE THAN 120 POUNDS IN HIS LIFE. WITH LITTLE FORMAL EDUCATION, LANCE NEVERTHELESS WAS the world authority on plant life in East Texas's Big Thicket. Botanists—"school doctors," Lance called them—came from as far away as South America, Japan, and France to be taught by the old man of the forest.

Lance would walk the famous scientists into the Big Thicket and teach them its way, correctly identifying sweet broom as *scopera adulcis* and magnolia as *glauca, acuminata,* or *florida.* Many of the scientists went away from the Big Thicket and wrote books and monographs on the wonder of it all, but few credited Lance with teaching them about that botanical marvel.

Lance Rosier lived in Saratoga, a small town up from the Texas coast before the beginning of Louisiana. North from there to the Oklahoma border is East Texas, and to understand East Texas you must know West Texas. An old cowboy, now long dead, once told me about East Texas, which he had never seen.

"Only thing wrong with East Texas," he said, "is . . . it confines a man. I like to see where I'm going tomorrow." He was holding the reins of his horse as we stood and talked on a ranch south of Amarillo in the Texas Panhandle and the land all around was flat and endless and treeless.

"Well, hell, son," he continued, "East Texas ain't no more'n West Texas, 'cept they got shade and we don't."

The old cowboy lived in the Texas of official record, that mythical country with its straight-line horizon and untenanted space. The legends of West Texas enriched Hollywood, and the common fantasy is that flat-bellied and lean-hipped John Waynes and Gary Coopers dwell there in boots and starched jeans, hats snugged low over dark, menacing eyes. Astride huge, white stallions they race across vastness like summer lightning and into our hearts off the cinema screen.

In West Texas bloom red and black and white cattle, wisps of smeared color on the gray landscape of a late afternoon.

Outlanders know that Texas by heart—and we Texans have gone to outlandish ends to create the myths—the boots-and-jeans stereotypes, smells of old leather and cattle, Cadillacs, and Neiman-Marcus suits for the Saturday night dance at the country club.

East Texas is something else. To begin with, the legends of East Texas are overalls; scents of dogwood and pine and fresh, green grass; Chevrolets and a blue serge from J. C. Penney's for the Saturday night dance at the American Legion Hall.

East Texas has no vastness, no endlessness. Its forests cause that, shutting you into cool, shady places, almost silent vacuums of flowers, pines, and ponds. So East Texas is seen in bits and pieces, like a jigsaw puzzle.

In West Texas you hear dry and twangy voices. The speech of East Texas is Southern-soft and solemn.

West Texans revere horses and cattle, huge ranches and oil wells. The East Texan, says a friend of mine, favors hound dogs—"dawgs"—and quiet fishing holes, small farms and oil wells. A West Texan does not mind driving 100 miles for a beer. An East Texan drinks his bourbon and branch in his rocking chair on the front porch.

In West Texas *the* tree is mesquite, an iron-skinned, thorny, and generally warped-trunk thing favored by shade-starved cows as a partial answer to the hot sun. East Texas has four national forests binding three-quarters of a million acres of pine, magnolia, oak, cypress, wild plum, black haw, bay, and sweet gum. There are thousands and thousands of privately owned forested acres, hiding sandy roads, natural pools of spring water, wild flowers, and peacefulness.

The trees cannot be overemphasized. If there is a boundary to East Texas, it is trees. West, north, or south, when the trees stop, East Texas is no more. And there, too, is the end of the Southern forests which reach all the way to the Atlantic.

"West Texas is a harsh, rude country and it needed harsh, rude men to settle there," I once heard a university professor say. "East Texas is softer, more gentle, and gentlemen were required to live with it."

In the 1600s the Spanish came, curious and conquering, claiming the land for kings who would never see it. Because God and the padres rode with them, they founded missions along a trail which crossed Texas at what now are Toledo Bend Reservoir, Sabine and Davy Crockett National Forests, the towns of San Augustine,

Nacogdoches, Alto, and Crockett, to San Antonio and, ultimately, to Mexico City.

El Camino Real, they called it. The King's Highway. French explorer René Robert Cavelier, Sieur de La Salle, later said the road was as much traveled as that "from Paris to Orleans." La Salle had claimed "all the country drained by the Mississippi . . . even to the mouth of the River of Palms," for King Louis XIV, after the Canadian trader's excursion down the Mississippi in 1682. Three years later, La Salle landed at Matagorda Bay, with 300 people and four ships, and founded Fort St. Louis. But things did not go well in the new settlement. Crops failed, supplies were diminished, and the Karankawas made life hazardous.

La Salle set out to find the Mississippi and go to France, via Canada, to seek help, but he was murdered by one of his men en route. Although his lieutenant, Henri Joutel, finally did reach France, he could not persuade Louis XIV to help the colony and within a short time, the settlement was destroyed by Indians.

There was no longer a French flag over Texas, but the Spaniards had been jolted by the establishment of Fort St. Louis. Suddenly they realized that unless they took possession of the Gulf Coast area, their claims to the region might be challenged repeatedly. Subsequent encroachment by other French settlers further motivated the Spanish to press the establishment of missions, forts, and villages throughout the East Texas we know today.

East Texans—the early ones—tended to cluster, creating hundreds of tiny settlements. Even today this region has no large cities as we think of them. Beaumont and Tyler are little more than large towns. Longview and Lufkin, Huntsville, Jacksonville, Palestine, and Marshall are trading centers, but small.

Beaumont attracted nationwide attention in January, 1901, with the discovery of the state's first oil gusher, in nearby Spindletop field. Up until then a lumbering town, Beaumont quickly became a bonanza town where there were fortunes to be made. In 1925 another oil pool at Spindletop proved even more productive than the first.

Long before oil became predominant, lumber and the cultivation of rice were major factors in the city's development. They still are.

The importance of East Texas's oil fields, combined with the creation of a 21-mile ship channel to the Gulf via Sabine Pass, has made Beaumont a vital part of the Golden Triangle, the mammoth industrial area that also includes Orange and Port Arthur.

Tyler, the municipal focal point of northern East Texas, is a pretty little city amid the pines, prosperous as a trading center, famed for its roses. There is no special reason, aside from fertile soil and reasonable climate, that the town began growing roses. Tyler struck it rich in the 1920s East Texas oil pool boom, after an inauspicious start in the 1840s. During the Civil War, nearby Camp Ford became the largest Union prisoner-of-war compound west of the Mississippi, and Marshall, a small town east of Tyler, served as state capital for the exiled Confederate government of Missouri.

By whatever means, the citizens of Tyler began cultivating roses, and the flowers today dominate the city.

They—and azaleas, which grow naturally in the pine forests—are everywhere. More than half the field-grown roses in America come from Tyler, and the municipal rose garden, which features over 400 varieties and 35,000 bushes, is one of the country's largest.

In mid-spring, when the roses and azaleas bloom in Tyler, the city celebrates with a tour of private homes and a flower show for thousands of visitors who come for the color and perfumed air.

Most of East Texas has been maintained as though suspended in time, a token of Americana that is too quickly disappearing: the small town. In East Texas are hamlets like Whitehouse and New London, New Boston, Lovelady, Holly Springs, and Camp Seale, and the lyrical litany of Tenaha, Timpson, Bobo, and Blair—the quartet of burgs was a railroad conductor's cry that became a famous craps-shooters' exhortation for World War I soldiers. Purists claim that East Texas stretches from Paris to Moscow, which is a kind of truth. The former is a town near the Oklahoma border, the latter is down near Houston.

Within those 26 eastern counties you may indeed travel from Paris to Moscow, and also to Bethlehem, Smyrna, Old Egypt, Malta, Macedonia, Klondike, Dixie, Detroit, and Warsaw. Not to mention Free Oneness, Hoot Index, Dime Box, Squeeze Penny School, Cut 'n Shoot, Shoe String (because that's what local oil wildcatters operated on), Tinrag (the Garnit family name spelled backward), Dimple, Squash Hollow, Gourd-Neck-or-Lick-Skillet, Carcass Hole, and the very poetical Sherry Prairie Cemetery.

Most today are no more than backwoods crossroads or a weather-worn general store but the names remain.

Like Dump. "I don't care what we call this dump as long as we get a post office," said an early settler. Frognot is Frognot because early residents killed all the frogs. Mutt and Jeff was named because the village's two leading merchants resembled those cartoon characters. Ambia, in Lamar County, is a name coined by a local justice of the peace to describe the amber jets of tobacco juice mouth-shot by town loafers.

Talco is the abbreviated name of the Texas, Arkansas and Louisiana Candy Company. Fink, where there is an annual international celebration for anyone named Fink (Finks have come from as far away as England), and Bug Tussle are a couple of famous East Texas names.

Karnack, birthplace of Lady Bird Johnson, was discovered by a local intellectual to be exactly the same distance from Caddo Lake as ancient Karnak in Egypt was from the Nile River, though the importance of such a coincidence is far from certain.

These villages, hidden away among the pines, are the sum and substance of East Texas. The area was settled by migrants from Tennessee and Arkansas and Alabama and other Southern states. One sociologist theorized, perhaps only partly in jest, that the farmers and families remained in East Texas and the malcontents, the unsociable men with dark, hard eyes and searching souls, traveled west to do battle with that unfortunate country. If West Texans would admit the truth, East Texas gave them everything they honor, except dust storms.

Above– MISSION TEJAS
Below– MIDWAY INN ON OLD SAN ANTONIO ROAD

Man generally has done well in East Texas. Author Mary Lasswell considered it a land of "caviar and clabber." Houston newspaper columnist Leon Hale claims East Texas is a place where men still dig their own fishing worms. In Hale's analysis is a profound abstraction but the superficial meaning is that East Texas is a good place to sit a spell.

I once sat for a long time in the parlor of the Excelsior House in Jefferson, which is one of those time-warp towns of East Texas. Much of Jefferson is preserved as it was a century ago, a cross-hatch of quiet streets and pleasant homes, many of them with state historic medallions hung beside their front doors and their architectural plans on file in the Library of Congress. There are homes with century-old beds and crystal chandeliers, and houses built by slaves, constructed of hand-made bricks baked in the sun.

Jefferson, on Caddo Lake, was a thriving steamboat town by the 1850s when boats from the Mississippi, coming by way of the Red and Sabine rivers, stopped with cargo and new settlers for Texas. The Great Red River Raft —geological name for the natural logjam that originally formed Caddo Lake—had created the watery passageway to landlocked Jefferson.

And Jefferson became prosperous. It was home to the famed Kelly Plow, which was invented and manufactured there, and the Blackburn Syrup Works. Texas's first gaslight system was installed in Jefferson, and the first ice plant. The state's first commercial beer was brewed in Jefferson and the first meeting in Texas of the Southern Baptist Convention was held there, although any connection between these historical facts is doubtful.

Jefferson's population boomed to 35,000 in 1870, and it was the wealthiest town in Texas. Jay Gould ended

LEGRANDE HOUSE, TYLER

all of that when he asked the city fathers for a right-of-way for his Texas and Pacific Railway. They replied that Jefferson was a riverboat town, not a railroad town, and Mr. Jay Gould could take his caboose elsewhere. He did, promising that grass would grow in Jefferson's streets. It did, because in time the logjam unjammed and drained away the town's riverboating fortunes.

Jefferson dwindled away beside Caddo Lake until a restoration program began in the early 1950s. Now much of the town is restored, with the Excelsior House and its comfortable parlor a centerpoint for all that was.

The century-old Excelsior has original furnishings in its rooms and it still is possible to sleep in beds that were occupied by Ulysses S. Grant, Rutherford B. Hayes, Jacob Astor, a Vanderbilt, Mr. Gould, and Oscar Wilde. There is even a specially built sleigh-bed, which a stoutly built matron had constructed to her proportions.

Jay Gould still is with Jefferson, perhaps as a reminder of what the town could have been had it accepted his offer of a railroad. Gould's private rail car sits across the street from the Excelsior. It was rescued decades ago from a siding near Pitner's Junction, another East Texas village. Restored, the 88-foot-long car speaks of the manner in which railroad lords once lived: It features a solid silver lavatory.

When I am in Jefferson I stroll to the old Oakwood Cemetery to visit the grave of Diamond Bessie and to read the ancient tombstones with their moralizing messages. One reads:

Remember, Friend, as you pass by,
As you are now, so once was I.
As I am now, so you must be,
Prepare for death and eternity.

HISTORIC HOME WITH MAGNOLIA, NACOGDOCHES

Once, local legend persists, a town wit charcoaled this addendum underneath:

Be still, my friend,
And rest content,
Until I find out
Just where you went.

Diamond Bessie's grave is in a shady nook of the cemetery. According to historians, she was Bessie Moore, who loved jewels, especially diamonds.

Bessie was a "beautiful but poor girl" whose ill fortune it was to fall in love with Abe Rothchild, the handsome son of a diamond merchant. The couple, Bessie bedecked in diamonds, came to Texas, to Jefferson, in 1877. One foggy Sunday they went into the forest to picnic. She was never seen alive again.

Abe was tried thrice before a jury finally acquitted him but Jeffersonians knew he was Bessie's murderer, and they commemorate her life and death in an annual drama with local actors. Bessie is depicted as a wronged woman, a tragic figure, although the truth was that she was a prostitute in Cincinnati and Little Rock before teaming up with Rothchild, to whom she probably was never married. Nevertheless, the synthetic tale of Diamond Bessie is acted out yearly in the little town beside the bayou.

The Big Cypress Bayou and Caddo Lake, the waterways through which hundreds of riverboats steamed into Jefferson, remain nearby, a world of eerieness largely unchanged today.

Caddo, with its swampy shores, its floating islands, the narrow serpentine channels winding through a jungle of trees draped with Spanish moss, is a mysterious creation in which lone boaters often become lost, though many of the major channels are marked with numbered posts to guide fishermen into and out of the bayou and lake. There is a Gothic serenity to the whole place, more evidence of the timelessness which holds East Texas.

I got lost once in East Texas, down by Votaw, and I never enjoyed anything more.

There are major highways, then paved side roads, then logging roads, and I drove onto a logging road deep within the pine forests to become lost. The road was one-lane bordered by grasses as high as my car's roof, and the forest was darkness punctuated by thin spirals of sunlight, like theater spotlights falling on the flowers of spring, the swamp buttercups and pink dogwood, blue flag iris and wild azalea.

It was early morning, soon after dawn, and I passed an old house made partly of logs, partly of poorly sawn planks. The living was gone out of the house and it was empty, dusty, and rotting inside. Shards of a rocker were scattered in one room. A dead house.

Through a window, beside the house, was a giant mass of pink-flowered rhododendrons, and trailing up the outside of the chimney was a vine of purple orchids. Wisteria was pushing onto the porch.

The forest was reclaiming the house and one day would absorb it, ingest it into the body of the land, and it would be gone.

Farther, I drove into a clearing and parked. I walked into the dark forest through the laser shafts of sunlight. There was no sky, only the roof of pines and hardwoods, and I had no feel for direction. At last I came to a tiny streamlet of fresh water, probably fed by a spring, and sat on a fallen log and let the morning's coolness seep in. I sat there for a long time, as though in an illusory copse of some lost world, and all the while, less than 100 miles away, earth-bound voices were speaking with men preparing to walk on the moon.

I returned to the car and continued on the logging road, coming finally to a paved highway, and turned left, toward what I perceived to be north. For almost an hour I drove. Morning fog lay in the sloughs, floated on the highway over streams, and then I drove into a shallow valley with heavier mists, and up into a town.

There was a square of stores and a massive, ornately sculptured rock courthouse with a grassy lawn and tall oaks draped with Spanish moss and waxy-leafed, white-flowering magnolia trees. Old men sat on cane-bottomed chairs under the oaks, playing dominoes and checkers, and children scrambled on the grass. Country women gathered in pairs and fours, their arms folded against themselves to fend off the coolness of the late morning.

The pastoral scene could have been taken from a woodcut of the last century, and my memory of the town square and the courthouse and the country folk is frozen on that moment. Years later, I tried again to find the little town but could not, and I wonder even today whether it was some kind of Brigadoon of the piney woods that comes to life only on spring mornings.

There are other towns like that within East Texas, smallish, bucolic, isolated by the splendor of the forest and time.

Northward from Houston there are 12 million forested acres secreting a lingering way of life alien to the rest of Texas, where, as Leon Hale once reported, Garrett's Snuff is as much a staple as flour, and mules are still traded as often as Fords, and there are alligators in the sloughs, and even Indians, the gentle Alabama-Coushattas, living on a reservation on the fringes of Lance Rosier's Big Thicket.

The Big Thicket once spread over 3 million acres, but to view the remains today you must drive east from Huntsville to Woodville, south to Kountz, west to Rye through Honey Island.

All about are bits and pieces of the Big Thicket, scraps of a lost ecological empire. The best estimate is that perhaps 300,000 acres remain of the thicket, and just 84,550 acres of that have been set aside as the Big Thicket National Preserve. The remainder has been left to land developers and logging companies.

Purists claim that the Big Thicket now exists only in tiny patches, some of which are no more than four acres in size. The thicket once spread across 11 counties, from Nacogdoches in the north to Beaumont in the south, and east and west from the Sabine to the Trinity River. But that has all changed. Take a droplet of mercury and strike it with a hammer. The mercury shatters into tinier beads. That is today's Big Thicket.

No other place in the world is like the Big Thicket.

There, three distinct climatic zones exist in harmony. A "biological crossroads," botanists have termed the thicket. Reindeer moss from the arctic grows beside desert cactus and the tropical palmetto. There are magnolia and 20 types of wild orchid and the High Plains mesquite and rhododendron such as thrives in the eastern Appalachians.

A botanical wonder, the Big Thicket spawns azaleas, great banks of honeysuckle and verbena, spider lilies and wild wisteria wherever they are allowed peace and sanctity from the bulldozer and chain saw. There are five carnivorous plants—plants which catch and feed on insects—known in the world. Four, the bog violet, sundew, bladderwort, and pitcher plant, are native to the Big Thicket.

Scientists speak of the Big Thicket as a "region of critical speciation," meaning that the climate, soil, and other botanical elements combine to create environmental change within plantlife. More than 100 different trees and plants grow and thrive in the thicket, and more than 300 species of birdlife. There is credible evidence that the ivory-billed woodpecker, long believed extinct, might still exist in the thicket of East Texas.

The Big Thicket, said Mary Lasswell, is a "giant, wild garden."

A century ago the Big Thicket of East Texas was a kind of isolated community in which hid families whose men did not want to involve themselves with the Civil War, and men with lawmen behind them fled into the mysterious reaches of the forest, living on possum and armadillos and alligators and fish from the streams. To flush this human prey, pursuers started fires and these "burnouts" still are visible within the thicket.

What really has happened to the Big Thicket since then is civilization.

Oil, perhaps, began the dissolution of the ecological miracle. Near Lance Rosier's home in Saratoga, in 1865, a farmer named John Fletcher Cotton dug the state's first oil well. He dug for the petroleum deposit after seeing his hogs covered with oil from seepage. Mules powered the drill bit.

A couple of years later, near the village of Chireno, two men found a trickle of oil from the banks of a stream. For a time they bottled oil from the stream as a lubricant for saddle and harness leather, but they wanted to expand their business. They drilled a hole eight inches wide and 70 feet deep to strike oil.

The well flowed 250 barrels of oil the first day, for the eons of warm, wet forests of East Texas had manufactured the largest petroleum pool in the United States.

If there is a moment in time when the fate of the Big Thicket was decided it was 10 a.m., January 10, 1901, when the Lucas well in the Spindletop field exploded in a 75,000-barrel shower, and the great Texas petroleum industry was born.

In the late 1920s, with Mr. Ford arming the country with Model T automobiles which fed on gasoline, the largest strike of American oil was discovered in upper East Texas.

For almost 40 years 4 billion barrels of oil were siphoned from that underground pool through 26,000 wells spread over 100,000 acres. In the city of Kilgore alone, more than 1,000 wells pumped day and night.

Still the oil pipelines are stripped into forest lands, and salt water overflows from wells to pollute streams and kill fish and disturb the pristine serenity of the thicket.

Conglomerate lumber and logging companies have also been painted as villains of the thicket. For their purposes it is better if the pines grow in straight rows without the random interference of hardwoods, such as the magnolia and beech. Lumber company scientists developed a hybrid pine that grew straight and tall, and quickly, and the pines were planted everywhere, growing in geometrically perfect rows with precise spacing, like corn in fields awaiting harvesting. The companies have been charged with systematically killing the hardwood trees. One company sprayed a brace of hardwoods with defoliant and killed an entire rookery of herons, egrets, and their young—and a pair of century-old magnolias, each more than 75 feet tall.

Conservationists long have lobbied for the creation of a national park to save the Big Thicket, but there is much local opposition to either a national park or preserve. Lumber and oil are major industries in East Texas, and employes fear their jobs will be lost with the establishment of public lands.

Loggers and oilmen were not the only intruders in the Big Thicket. Ranchers found the grasses of East Texas sweeter and more abundant and cattle-raising began. In lower East Texas rice farmers drained the sloughs. And city dwellers, to escape the megalopoli in which they labored for five exasperating days, became willing customers for weekend retreat homes in the cool, uncomplicated forests of East Texas.

It is useless to dwell on what might have been for the Big Thicket. It mostly is gone now, and whether the strewn niblets of a national preserve will save the remainder is speculative masochism.

Once I walked with Lance Rosier into his forest. Then, in the mid-1960s, the thicket still had presence, still was awesome in its size and a biological island. With Lance leading, we wandered through palmetto groves, and tramped in the spongy earth over streams and into dark recesses of vines and fallen, rotting logs.

After an hour we paused on the edge of a clearing and gazed at the Witness Tree, soaring like a sentinel above the lesser surrounding oaks and beeches, sweet gums and pines.

That was, Lance told me, the largest magnolia tree in the world. A year or so later I read that someone had bored holes in its trunk and injected poisons into the tree. The Witness Tree was dead, the victim of the still volatile controversy between those who would preserve the Big Thicket and those who think that eliminating the hardwoods would put an end to talk of conserving the thicket.

The magnolia was a thousand years old when it was murdered.

HILL COUNTRY

T**HE HILL COUNTRY IS A PLACE OF ROLLING ROCKY HILLS AND OAK THICKETS, THIN CLEARWATER CREEKS AND SPRINGS, WHERE THE SPRING INFUSION OF BLUEBONNETS AND INDIAN BLANKET IS MOST DRAMATIC, PERHAPS** because of the quiet serenity of the countryside.

LBJ Country, it was called, when "He" was alive and living there on his Pedernales River ranch, when "He" was president and the second White House was his compact home beside a flower-banked stream.

Because of clean, clear air and a moderate climate, several environmental studies have bestowed upon the Texas Hill Country the title of America's most healthy region, a designation that lures retirees, artists, and city dwellers who dream of escaping to a slower way of life.

There are no large cities within the Hill Country, only small towns and villages, and no freeways and Interstate Highways, but narrow paved roads that curve and dip over the hills and into the small valleys. Austin, the state capital, on the eastern edge, and San Antonio, at the southern edge, are anchors for the area. But mostly the Hill Country contains small ranches and farms and has a bucolic way of life that is both contagious and enduring.

In spring when the bluebonnets are spread on the pastures, the roads fill with automobiles as Texans drive into their Hill Country. Last season's home-canned jams and jellies and early fruit and vegetables fill roadside stands. Artists and quilt-makers lay out their wares on courthouse lawns. Deer bound over the hills and wild turkeys nest in the oak thickets, scissortail mockingbirds soar playfully above the streams. Spring is a regenerative time in the Hill Country.

Because the Balcones Fault held its underground vaults of spring water, Central Texas from the beginning was settled by farmers, Germans mostly, who gave an assiduous stability to the area, but other nationalities came, too.

The French settled in Castroville along the Medina River. Homes there still have the look of those built by Alsatian pioneers. Panna Maria is certified as the oldest Polish community in North America. Canary Islanders founded Floresville.

The Balcones Fault divides the coastal plains and the Edwards Plateau, a steppe of thin-soiled limestone as much as 10,000 feet thick and the rising staircase to West Texas. Because of shallow soil, the outer edge of the Hill Country contains thriving ranches but few farms. The light rainfall and dry air create conditions for spectacular lightning storms in August and September, a summer phenomenon that never fails to stun and awe those travelers who witness the night sky displays.

The Hill Country was, at one time, the frontier of western America, and in the years following statehood soldiers there built a north-to-south picket line of forts and posts, continuing the country's policy of Manifest Destiny.

The land was once owned and ruled by the Comanches, those prairie centaurs who had dominated West Texas since they captured Spanish ponies and learned to ride. The Comanches even defeated the conquistadores in 1758, a year after they built a mission, San Saba de la Santa Cruz, near what now is the town of Menard. More than 2,000 Indians attacked. The Spanish left and never returned, and today the mission/fort's stone foundations beside the San Saba River are very nearly all that remain of the conquistadores' presence in Central Texas.

At other western posts nearby, the U.S. Army conducted an outlandish experiment in the 1850s. One hundred and twenty camels were imported from Smyrna, with a dozen Turkish and Syrian camel drivers, to test the humped animals in Texas's waterless desert.

Headquartered at present-day Kerrville, the camels and their reluctant U.S. soldier-riders were sent on reconnaissance expeditions as far away as the Big Bend. The general consensus of historians is that the camels succeeded, the soldiers failed. The camels survived on almost no water and even ate the acidic creosote bush, while the soldiers cussed and kicked the beasts and never accepted their new role in the Camel Corps.

The Civil War doomed the experiment. The soldiers returned east to fight and the camels were abandoned to wander loose in the west. Many were shot by frontiersmen frightened by the strange animals. Others were captured and used as beasts of burden. Still others served as curiosities in traveling carnivals into the early 20th century. Many of the imported camel handlers remained in the United States. One of them migrated to Mexico where his son, Plutarco Elias Calles, became president in the middle 1920s.

An irony of the failed American Camel Corps is that it headquartered in Texas's best-watered region, where rivers stream out of the limestone and cut through the hills. The San Saba, the Llano, the Nueces, the Sabinal, the Frio, the Guadalupe, the Comal, the San Marcos—all flow through the Hill Country, often bordered by cypress and fed by springs.

The Comal, about three miles long, is said to be the shortest river carrying a large volume of water in the United States. It rises in the town of New Braunfels, and its swiftness makes it perfect for tubing excursions. Rushing springs form the headwaters of the San Marcos River, and on a small lake at Aquarena Springs, a family theme park, there are glass-bottom boats for viewing fish and plant life.

The Colorado River dissects the Hill Country and is dammed almost to extinction, though the elongated lakes formed through the region provide splendid scenic and recreation centers. The Highland Lakes—a half-dozen sleek bodies of water set like stepping stones down the spine of the Hill Country—reach into the city limits of Austin.

Austin, the state capital, is a graceful, soft city, the western edge of which is rumpled with beginnings of those rolling hills. Once it was called Waterloo. To escape the malarial swamps of Houston, politicians sought a new capital site. In 1839 a commission appointed by Texas President Mirabeau B. Lamar chose Waterloo because "the imagination of even the romantic will not be disappointed in viewing the valley of the Colorado [River] and the fertile and gracefully undulating woodlands and luxuriant prairies at a distance from it." They named the city Austin, for early Texas colonizer Stephen F. Austin.

Governmental records were moved from Houston that same year by 50 oxen-hauled wagons. But the commission had been duped by settlers who failed to tell about the marauding Indians and bands of Mexican outlaws. With the establishment of Austin as headquarters for the Republic of Texas, it was hoped that the raiders would be forced away. Eventually they were, but a stockade protected the first capital as late as 1845.

A university city, Austin has half-a-dozen excellent museums, including Formosa, the studio of sculptress Elizabet Ney, whose art works are on display around the world. She was a formidable woman. Ney, born in Germany, arrived in Hempstead in 1873 with her husband, Dr. Edmund Montgomery, to whom she sometimes pretended she was not married. As described by a contemporary, she wore a Grecian robe bound with a golden chain and her throat was circled with a diamond necklace given her by the King of Prussia. One arm was adorned with a bracelet, the gift of Queen Victoria, and on the other wrist was a circlet of diamonds and emeralds bestowed by George V of Hanover.

Her appearance among the Texas pioneers clad in homemade duds spun of coarse cloth created more than a little curiosity. Ney's acceptance in the community was not strengthened when she strapped on two six-guns with

her Grecian gown and rode horseback across her lands. Later she moved to Austin, to the mansion she named Formosa, and there she sculpted while wearing Turkish bloomers and a turban. Only her fame and skill as an artist saved her from public condemnation.

Texas's capitol, intentionally made taller by seven feet than the U.S. capitol, is of course the center of the city. The domed rotunda, 309 feet and eight inches from the bottom floor, supports what one historian called the "ugliest 16-foot-tall statue of the Goddess of Liberty in the world." A state archivist once declared that the statue was an unattractive granite-faced sentinel for Texas.

She rises there above the dome, sword in one hand, the Star of Texas in the other, and no one is really sure where she came from. There are no records, except a faded photograph of workers preparing to hoist her to her dome perch, and newspaper clippings from February 26, 1888, stating that she was in place.

The capitol was built for $3 million in what must be one of the strangest financing deals on record. Almost bankrupt, the State of Texas traded 3 million acres of land in the Texas Panhandle to a syndicate headed by two Chicago brothers, John V. and C. B. Farwell, who, with British financial backing, agreed to build Texas a state capitol in exchange.

The capitol was constructed of granite mined from quarries near Marble Falls, while the Farwells were establishing the world's largest ranch—the XIT—on land most Texans considered uninhabitable and as distant and alien as Turkestan. The dollar-an-acre land, however, proved to be a boon for the Farwells, who eventually subdivided it and sold their vast spread for millions of dollars.

Austin is the home of the Lyndon Baines Johnson Presidential Library, on the campus of the University of Texas. It houses the late president's private papers, memorabilia of his long public career, and an exact replica of the White House Oval Office.

LBJ, it was noted on the occasion of the library's opening, "was, doubtless, the last president whose roots and early experiences would bridge the gap between the old America of local frontiers, crossroads, and close neighbors, and the new America of world power, big cities, and unknown neighbors." His archives are in Austin, but his birthplace and his ranch are 40 miles west in Stonewall.

The Lyndon B. Johnson National Historic Site and State Historical Park is composed of two units. The LBJ Ranch Unit, in Stonewall, includes the family home, his log cabin birthplace, and a reconstructed schoolhouse where Johnson first attended classes in 1912. LBJ is buried in the family cemetery under giant oaks beside the slow-moving Pedernales River.

Thirteen miles east, in the Johnson City Unit, is his small frame boyhood home, which still contains many of the family's original furnishings.

Lady Bird Johnson is honored in nearby Fredericksburg, where a 190-acre park bears her name, but this small Hill Country town, perhaps the region's favorite, has other attributes as well.

Fredericksburg is the most German village of Central Texas. Along with New Braunfels, the town first was settled in 1846 by German immigrants. Plagued by disease and attacked by Indians, they signed a peace treaty with the Comanches in 1847 to insure the survival of their settlement, and began farming.

Their legacy is an architecture of the last century, a population which still speaks German in many homes, restaurants with sauerkraut and wurst-based meals, and the 130-year-old Steamboat Hotel, whose register contains the names of such historic individuals as Ulysses S. Grant and Robert E. Lee.

The hotel was bought by Charles Nimitz, a German settler who added a ship's bridge and superstructure that inspired the name. His grandson was Chester Nimitz, last of America's five-star admirals and a World War II hero.

Now part of the Admiral Nimitz Center, the hotel serves as a museum for the Pacific Fleet commander's war mementoes and papers. Included in the Center is the Garden of Peace, which was designed and funded by the Japanese people.

The German heritage of Fredericksburg melds nicely with other pioneer traditions, especially the annual Easter Fires Pageant, which attracts thousands of onlookers each year. How the story began is unknown. Tradition says it was first told by a pioneer mother whose children were frightened by fires on hillsides surrounding Fredericksburg. Those spring fires, the mother told her children, were lighted by the Easter rabbit, who used them to cook and color the eggs which are found in Easter baskets. In reality, the bonfires were tended by fierce Comanches keeping a wary eye on the first settlers of the village.

The Indians usually set up their hillside fire watches after worshipping at Enchanted Rock, north of Fredericksburg. That massive granite outcropping covers 640 acres and is second in size only to Stone Mountain in Georgia. Prehistoric Texans may have performed rituals of human sacrifice on the 500-foot-tall rock. The Indians who named it believed the rock was inhabited by gods, to whom they prayed and left food offerings.

Enchanted Rock long has been a prominent Central Texas landmark. It rises beside Sand Creek amid the oak thickets and is a pleasant weekend excursion site. Families can walk up trails and picnic on the summit, from which a view of the surrounding landscape can be seen from horizon to horizon. Religious services are still observed atop the granite hill from time to time, much as they were a century ago.

Within Texas, the Hill Country is an island of creeks and rolling, timbered ranchlands. Outside Austin, the pines of the East Texas woods give way to the scrub oaks and hardwoods of lower West Texas. North, toward Waco, the land flattens for farming and dairying and is crossed by a major river, the Brazos. And south, beyond the Nueces River, is found the brush country, the barren, iniquitous land the Mexicans called the *brasada*.

VEREINS KIRCHE, FREDERICKSBURG

Above– UNIVERSITY OF TEXAS, AUSTIN
Below– AUSTIN SKYLINE AND COLORADO RIVER
Right– GOVERNOR'S MANSION, AUSTIN

Left– CASCADE ON GUADALUPE RIVER
Below– FENCE AND PASTURE OF BROOMWEED NORTH OF MERIDIAN

Below– GRANITES OF THE LLANO UPLIFT AT BALANCED ROCK
Right– LIMESTONE CLIFF, UPPER GUADALUPE RIVER
Overleaf– BLUEBONNETS AND MESQUITE, ENNIS

Above– ARKANSAS YUCCA AND WHITE BUCKWHEAT, SALADO
Below– CANYON LAKE AND OAKS ON DEVIL'S BACKBONE
Right– GRASSY PLAIN, MERIDIAN

WHERE The WEST BEGAN

THE PECOS RIVER HAS BRACKISH WATER SOURED WITH ALKALINE FROM THE MEAN AND MARVELOUS LAND THROUGH WHICH IT FLOWS. *RIO DE LAS VACAS*—RIVER OF COWS—WAS AN EARLY SPANISH NAME FOR THE STREAM BE-cause, curdled though its water may have been, it was water nonetheless, and wild cattle drank from the stream to sustain life.

The Pecos enters the Rio Grande as the latter turns north after forming the Big Bend. Replenished by the sourish water of the Pecos, the Rio Grande again veers southeast toward the Gulf of Mexico.

Between the Pecos and the Gulf are the northern and eastern remnants of the Chihuahuan Desert, the *brasada,* which leaps the Rio Grande to impose its malicious disposition on Texas. "It was either swept with gray dust borne on blistering winds or beaten by deluges that hissed as they first struck the hot ground or raked by blizzards that came whistling out of the north," wrote historian Paul Horgan of the *brasada.*

A land of hard secrets, he called the brush country, and every living thing inside fought for its place. There were mesquite, both brush and tree, with barbed thorns; *huisache,* with bright yellow blooms; the catclaw, called "wait-a-minute" by Mexicans, because it grabs at men's arms and legs; and hillocks of prickly pear cactus, which looked to O. Henry like ". . . large, fat hands."

In spring the yucca, or Spanish dagger, blooms in the *brasada.* Its central ridgepole stalk, often rising 20 feet above the desert, stands like a ship's spar over the laby-rinthine tortuous Eden, tipped by a puffy explosion of white blossoms. Early travelers through the brush country guided themselves by the blooming yucca, moving through the maze of interlocking thickets from blossom to blossom like sailors guided by stars at sea. Trails through the *brasada* often dead-ended and few men knew a safe route through.

The brush country was an asylum for the angry misanthropes of nature, the rattlesnake, black bears, the savage peccary, and the Longhorn. Within the brush country, though, two American institutions were born—the cattle industry and the cowboy.

From the Spanish, men had gotten horses and cattle,

and from Mexican vaqueros came the paraphernalia of cowboying—sombrero, lariat, horned saddle, boots, spurs. It was for the *brasada* that the vaqueros devised the leather leggings we call chaps, for without them men were bloodied as they sought safe passage across that evil place. From the vaquero also arose the animist trinity of cow/horse/land that formed the basis of the myth of The West.

The wild Longhorn was a preposterous beast. In its brush country sanctuary, wrote J. Frank Dobie, chronicler of the Southwest, the Longhorn was "a parody of a cow."

"It had elk legs," wrote another historian of the animal that created a cattle empire, "and could outrun a horse, was bony, high at the shoulders, low at the tail, shaggy-haired, gaunt-rumped, with a goat-limber neck holding a massive head from which grew horns curved like twin scimitars."

The Longhorn sustained itself on wind and water, early superstitious cowboys believed. Evolved from strayed Moorish cattle brought to the New World by the Spanish, Longhorns in the wild feared nothing, and if provoked would attack anything, even the black bears and especially wary cowboys who came with lariats to rope and drag them out of the brush.

With no herd instinct, the untamed Longhorn bull—often a brute of 1,200 pounds standing as high as a man on horseback—maintained a few wives for which he was an aggressive protector.

"At sunset," it has been written of the Longhorn, "he called his family together for the night and his bel-low, heard by cowboys camped in the *brasada,* was fear-some, chilling—the roar of a true wild beast."

The Longhorn was never civilized. It was chased down, dragged to corrals, herded, branded, conditioned to a gentler environment, but never tamed. At best, cowboy and Longhorn regarded one another during those early years of western American history with a certain apprehension.

Captured within the *brasada* and forced to accept an anxious truce with man, the Longhorns multiplied and spread throughout Texas. After the Civil War, the north was beef-starved. Texas had beef, but no market. The only answer was to herd the beeves to the north, across a thousand miles of open land to railheads in Kansas where the cattle could be shipped to Chicago, butchered, and sold in the east. A Longhorn worth $2 in Texas was suddenly worth $30 in Kansas. Ranchers in deep South Texas formed up the first long-distance cattle drives.

"Them Longhorns," recalled an Oklahoma rancher of this century, "could live on nothing, and you could drive them to market and it didn't hurt 'em because they wasn't any good to begin with."

Today the Texas Longhorn, supplanted on the prairies by fatter, more tractable cattle, is a living anachronism, a surly antique kept by a few ranchers to remind them of the past. The *brasada,* though crossed by highways, remains a fierce place of brush and heat and wilderness. Like the Longhorn, it has never been tamed.

There were numerous trails north from Texas worn to dust by the hooves of 10 million cattle in the decade after the Civil War. A major one—the Dodge Trail—traversed the Red River near present-day Vernon. Another, the Chisholm, began in deep South Texas and bore north for Wichita and Abilene.

Richard King, a former riverboat captain, was one of the first to push his Longhorn herds to Kansas railheads. King founded a ranching empire that still flourishes on the eastern edge of Texas's brush country. He owned a million acres of grassland on the Gulf coastal plain that became the King Ranch. King once seriously considered buying a strip of land from South Texas to Kansas, fencing it so he could drive his cattle across a thousand miles of his own property.

Where the trails, the cattle, and the cowboys went, settlements grew wealthy. The first major barrier to the Chisholm was the Brazos River. A settlement already existed on the Brazos when the first cattlemen reached there. A Scotsman, Neil McLennan, and an Austrian, George Erath, surveyed the river crossing in 1840, and a Jamaican, Jacob de Cordova, laid out the first town plats.

There was a ferry across the river for travelers, but the cattle had to swim and that was a tiring, lengthy job. While the cowboys waited, they frequented the town's saloons and raised hell, which caused the village to be named Six-Shooter Junction.

Later, when more peaceful travelers arrived, the settlement was renamed Waco, for the region's Hueco Indians. A Texas Ranger fort was built to protect townspeople from the Indians. Colleges were begun—Baylor University, oldest continuous institution of higher education in Texas, is still one of the state's largest. In 1870 what was then the world's longest suspension bridge was built across the Brazos. (New York's Brooklyn Bridge was patterned after the span in Waco, probably because the same man, August Roebling, designed both.)

Waco has become a university city still served by the river—the excursion sternwheel *Brazos Queen* plies its waters daily. Baylor's Armstrong Browning Library houses the world's largest collection of works by Robert and Elizabeth Barrett Browning. And the lore of the Texas Rangers is preserved in the frontier-style buildings of the Texas Ranger Hall of Fame and the Homer Garrison Memorial Museum.

And so the Brazos was crossed, and as the vast herds continued northward the cowboys passed the last bit of civilization before reaching the wilderness of Oklahoma Territory: Fort Worth.

Because Fort Worth lay where south-to-north cattle drives met east-to-west Manifest Destiny, the town suffered with all the substantive elements of The West: a marvelous shopping mall of sin called Hell's Half Acre, railroads in all directions, buffalo hunters, the cavalry, lynchings, redeye whiskey, wagon trains, stagecoaches to Yuma, cattle stampedes, and dusty street gunfights.

For many years Fort Worth bore the burden of the slogan "Where The West Begins." But if you would find an actual physical beginning to The West, look on the far side of a hundred-mile-wide band of good farming land called Cross Timbers. West of Fort Worth and Cross Timbers, the soil changes from rich browns and blacks to beige sands, pale red clays. Mesquites replace oaks. The land no longer rolls but is levelness punctuated with ragged-topped knolls, sloping upward to the sun.

The West began out there, in a vast expanse that now is called West Texas, an area of some 250,000 square miles. The legends that captivated Saturday matinee audiences and established the cowboy as a Homeric character were created out on that dusty savanna.

The cowboy, said historian Horgan, was "the last of the clearly traditional characters [born] from the kind of land he worked in and the kind of work he did."

Fiction, especially celluloid fiction, transposed the cowboy into a sort of paladin of the sagebrush, but the truth is harsher. One writer characterized the western cowboy this way:

> He neither built nor explored nor populated the west but moved ever so briefly across it, as capricious and lonely as the blowing dust. Dime novelists and penny dreadful authors scribbled magniloquent lies about the cowboy for rapt Eastern readers, but saw him only in town, often ending long cattle drives with a few desperate hours of extravagant carousal before returning to a life of social desolation. Like a cloistered monk of some distant forgotten monastery, the cowboy served his god, the rancher, and toiled at labors decidedly unglamorous. Moving often from ranch to ranch, the cowboy made few lasting friendships. He was untutored and ignorant. For endless months he lived on the range, burned in summer, frozen in winter, as punished as the cattle he attended. . . . He lived in a society of men, and made love to the only available women, the ubiquitous "soiled doves" and "fallen angels," on almost a seasonal basis, like some animal in heat. He smelled of the horse he rode, of the cows he tended, and the dung of both. Miasmic as a nocturne, the cowboy was a neutered man, often profane, never profound, illiterate, itinerant. . . . His was a "soulless, aimless" existence, wrote one of the few introspective cowboys who left the range world when he saw it for what it was.

The cowboy, however transliterated into a phantasmagorian personality, died with The West and the life span of each was much shorter than the legends have led us to believe.

In 1876 a 21-year-old salesman named John Gates came to San Antonio's Military Plaza with rolls of strange wire. He strung the wire, studded with sharp-pointed barbs, onto posts and challenged cowmen to drive their cattle through it.

"This is the finest fencing in the world," he shouted, "light as air, stronger than whiskey, cheaper than dirt, all steel, and a yard wide."

The demonstration convinced Texas cattlemen. They bought the barbed wire, ending forever the era of open ranges, and coincidentally making the young man a fortune. He became known as "Bet-A-Million" Gates.

The West lived no more than two decades, perhaps less. There was a prologue and epilogue, but generally The West began with cattle drives after the Civil War and ended in San Antonio with the introduction by Gates of that remarkable wire. The rest is anticlimactic.

Barbed wire closed the free ranges and localized ranching operations. The railroad moved west, ending the need for trail drives. It became safer, albeit less profitable, to sell cattle at nearby railheads. Herefords and Angus cattle were introduced and the obsolete Longhorn was bred away into oblivion. Without the need for vast acreage, ranchers began selling off pieces of their land to settlers, and the cowboy, that unfettered, allodial child of the range, disappeared from all but the silver screen or the pages of pulp fiction. The likes of him will never be with us again.

The cowboy of today is a far different creature, found only on the very largest ranches, which can afford to hire a man for bed and found. If he rides the range at all, it is in a pickup truck, and his gear—boots, ten-gallon hat, kerchief, lariat, chaps—largely are symbolic of a lost age. His cowboying labors in this century mostly are fence and windmill repairs because today even most cattle are gone from the range, and are raised in vast feedlots like hothouse vegetables.

Time slew The West.

SEPARATING HERD

Above– CATTLE AT WINDMILL WATER TANK
Below– RODEO SCENE
Right– HEREFORDS IN CORRAL

PRAIRIE, PLAINS, and PANHANDLE

DALLAS IS NOT THE WEST. "THE NEW YORK OF TEXAS," DALLAS HAS BEEN CALLED. IT IS THE LEAST TYPICAL OF TEXAS'S PRINCIPAL CITIES, AND THE IRONY IS THAT DALLAS SHARES A VAST PIECE OF THE STATE'S NORTHern plains with Fort Worth, Texas's most stereotypical city. Together with surrounding satellite municipalities, Dallas/Fort Worth is the Metroplex, a statistical megalopolis with an area larger than the states of Connecticut and Rhode Island combined, a hundred-mile-long city whose total population would make it America's third or fourth largest metropolis.

But Dallas and Fort Worth are unlikely to be joined. They exist alongside one another, separate and unequal, often mutually uncooperative, and the perfect specimen of the dichotomy defining Texas in the 1980s.

Fort Worth began in 1849 as an army post to protect settlers on the frontier of western America. Almost at the same time, 30 miles to the east, a trading post was built beside the Trinity River. The trading post became Dallas. For more than a century the cities have shared the Trinity River, a shallow contorted little stream, and the flatness—the Grand Prairie—that separates East and West Texas. There has ever been a civic rivalry, sometimes fierce, sometimes silly and petty, but much of that has disappeared as the cities have matured.

Dallas and Fort Worth have been linked by suburbia, and though their downtowns are 27 miles apart, they are virtually one on the North Texas prairie, separate but coupled, the same yet different. Perhaps the division is geographic. Dallas sits with its tall buildings and merchandising talents on the fringe of Texas's pine forests. Fifty miles east the pines begin and run to Georgia. Fort Worth's skyline overlooks a westward-rolling grassland, the front yard of legendary Texas, the oil well, Cadillac, jackrabbit, and cowboy empire. One must live in Texas all his life not to be startled by the topographic schizophrenia of Dallas and Fort Worth.

Dallas is more cosmopolitan, sleeker. Fort Worth is more western, folksy. Dallas wooed and won eastern financiers; Fort Worth was a prime saloon stop on the famed Chisholm Trail and a departure point for emigrants moving west. Dallas became a merchandising mecca;

Fort Worth built a stockyard conglomerate second only to Chicago's. They were never twin cities on the plains but a pair of disparate towns 27 miles and poles apart, rent by the 97th meridian and all logic. That tight slab of range could not support two big rich cities and Fort Worth early was cast in the lesser role because it played on a barren stage to a destitute West Texas while larger Dallas sought a more sophisticated audience.

Even today, the difference is notable. Dallas is touted as the future Texas, a chic, worldly place. Fort Worth is described as Texas's most typically western city, home of the cowboy. The distinct personality of each city is most obvious in some recent comparisons: Richard Burton bought Elizabeth Taylor a diamond in Dallas; actor Jimmy Stewart bought his wife a registered bull in Fort Worth. Princess Grace did her haute couture shopping in Dallas and purchased ten cases of barbecued beans in Fort Worth. Parisian designer Yves St. Laurent showed his latest fashions in Dallas but bought western shirts off the rack in Fort Worth. Damon Runyon once characterized this Eastern/Western schism: "In Dallas, the women wear high heels. In Fort Worth, the men do."

Whatever their past, Dallas and Fort Worth are awash with renaissance, with rediscovery. As a pivotal metropolis in what economists and sociologists are calling the Sunbelt, these cities are luring new settlers in record numbers. They come as much for the lifestyle as the opportunity.

Stanley Marcus, of the famed Neiman-Marcus specialty stores, once defined life in Dallas/Fort Worth: "Other locales seem to deal in fashion. Here, we deal in style. It's the difference between the superficial and the actual, between the transitory and the eternal." What he was saying was, Dallas and Fort Worth live well.

Dallas soars with a concrete-and-steel skyline built of banking, insurance, fashion, film making, and electronics. Second in size only to Houston, Dallas is more cultured and conservative than the Gulfport city, and has reached the 1980s with a studied superiority in the performing arts. The Dallas Theatre Center, home of the only theater designed by Frank Lloyd Wright, has a national reputation for excellence; it has concentrated on presenting new works by Texans and other southwestern playwrights. The city's opera, symphony, and ballet companies are consistently ranked among America's best.

At the western edge of downtown, amid those rising skyscrapers, is a bit of historic Dallas, the preserved log cabin trading post, now adjacent to the infamous School Book Depository, grassy knoll, and underpass—the site of President John F. Kennedy's assassination.

The JFK Memorial is a block away, a simple, tasteful park with a somber obelisk commemorating that sad day in November, 1963.

Dallas has preserved other bits and pieces of its history. Old City Park, the first park in Dallas, now serves as a kind of outdoor museum. "An old-age home for venerable buildings," remarked one visitor. Restorations in the park include a farmer's log cabin from 1847, a Victorian mansion, a school, a church, a railroad depot, a doctor's office, and a small hotel. All are authentic and compose a picturesque window on Texas's past.

Both Dallas and Fort Worth have developed cultural centers. The Dallas complex evolved around Fair Park, built for the Texas Centennial celebration in 1936 and still the site of the annual state fair, largest in the nation.

On its grounds is the exceptionally well-stocked Museum of Fine Arts, with a peerless collection of North American art, ranging from exquisite Indian gold work to pre-Columbian and pre-Christian-era statuary and pottery.

Nearby are the Museum of Natural History, the Health and Science Museum, the Aquarium, and a garden center filled with exotic plantings from around the world.

While Dallas was establishing itself as a performing arts city, Fort Worth concentrated on museums. Its cultural center, on the near west side, has acquired a worldwide reputation, especially the Kimbell Art Museum, which has been ranked among the best in America.

Housed in an award-winning, almost surrealistic building designed by famed Philadelphia architect Louis Kahn, the Kimbell is a stunning museum. It is countersunk into a nine-acre park and blends so well with the surroundings that it seems small, but actually is longer than a football field. To diminish its interior size, Kahn tucked away pocket gardens, courtyards, and areas with comfortable furniture where visitors may sit among the art works. "It is," Kahn explained, "a friendly home in which to enjoy art."

The collection, assembled by the museum's original director, the late Richard Fargo Brown, is not large. But critics have acclaimed it as magnificent. Works by Rembrandt and Degas, El Greco, Picasso, Matisse, Hals, Murillo, Goya, and Gainsborough are included. The museum actually spans 5,000 years of art, displaying gold and silver Persian plates; a Cambodian Buddha; a medieval wood panel altarpiece; an exquisite apse from a small French chapel; even a Bellini painting once owned by Napoleon (the work disappeared more than a hundred years ago and was not seen again until the Kimbell opened; Brown would not reveal where he discovered the painting).

The Kimbell joins the Amon G. Carter Museum of Western Art, the Fort Worth Art Center, and the Museum of Science and History on Carter Square, a compact civic center which also includes Casa Mañana, a summer musical theater, and the Will Rogers Memorial Auditorium/Coliseum, behind which are the massive cattle barns where the city stages its annual Fat Stock Show and Rodeo, one of the oldest in America.

The Amon G. Carter Museum is considered one of the best museums of western Americana in the country, and is perhaps the premier repository of paintings by Frederic Remington and Charles M. Russell. Those works are the heart of the museum's collection, which covers all of North America's frontier history, from the time Pilgrims landed to the continent's final settlement in the Far West.

The museum also maintains a microfilm collection of early western newspapers and an extensive library, both of which are available to qualified scholars. More than a dozen important books have come out of the Carter Museum research facilities.

The Carter Museum tells the story of the Old West. And Fort Worth still retains much of its frontier heritage. Remains of that time are visible on the city's north side in the vast stockyards area, where boots and jeans still are daily work clothes.

Streets around that part of town have wooden storefronts. There is a weekly rodeo and a cattle auction. Restaurants and bars continue to cater to the cowboys and ranchers who come to Fort Worth from West Texas.

The only entity really shared by Dallas and Fort Worth is the regional airport, America's largest. It is important to note that the airport, more than 18,000 acres, is precisely equidistant between the two cities.

It is also essential to point out that although the world knows the megalopolis as the "Dallas/Fort Worth Metroplex," on the western end of that hundred-mile-long urban sprawl the term is written "Fort Worth/Dallas."

Midway between Cross Timbers and the New Mexico mountains is a sudden rocky cliff, the Cap Rock, a natural limestone escarpment and stepping-stone from the brushy roughness of lower West Texas onto the High Plains.

America's Great Plains begin at the Cap Rock, which rises as much as a thousand feet and curls south, then west, into New Mexico. In Texas, the grassy flatland was called *Llano Estacado*, the Staked Plain, and when Coronado came in 1541, it was treeless, level, and seemingly as endless as the Russian Steppes.

For more than 200 years the Plains and Panhandle saw few white men. The Comanches ruled the land amid limitless herds of buffalo and elk.

Buffalo hunters were the first real invaders of the Plains and Panhandle, and they literally destroyed the Indians' way of life. Millions of buffalo were slaughtered, their hides dried and shipped to railheads in Fort Worth.

It was not until the 1870s that settlement began, after the Army finally had conquered the Plains Indians, a few hundred remaining Comanche and Kiowa and Cheyenne who had waged a three-decade war against any intrusion into their domain.

When the end came in 1874, in Cito Canyon at Palo Duro, the resolution of that long war was simple in its execution. Plains Indians were the finest horsemen in the world, and among the best guerrilla fighters. In the au-

tumn of 1874, the largest surviving band came to camp in Palo Duro. Shortly before a late September dawn, the Fourth Cavalry of Colonel Ranald Mackenzie attacked, and chased away the Indians' corraled horses. Without their horses, the Indians were impotent, virtually helpless, and soon they were captured and interned on Oklahoma reservations. Except for isolated incidents by a few renegades, the Texas Plains had been pacified. The killing of buffalo, too, ended in that watershed year of 1874, the herds having been all but wiped out.

The last major Indian encounter had occurred three months earlier at Adobe Walls, a buffalo hunter encampment northeast of Amarillo. The crude mud hut fort was attacked by 700 Indians, who hoped to wipe out the white hunters. Twenty-eight hunters, among them Bat Masterson, repelled the attack with their Sharps long rifles. The Indians put the fort under siege for five days. It was on the third day that Billy Dixon recorded the longest rifle kill in frontier history. Dixon shot a Cheyenne chieftain from a distance later measured at seven-eighths of a mile.

Ranchers and settlers slowly began arriving on the Plains. Charles Goodnight, who with his partner Oliver Loving had pioneered the Goodnight-Loving Trail up the Pecos Valley to cattle markets in New Mexico, was the first rancher in that harsh compound, headquartering in the colorful Palo Duro Canyon, south of Amarillo.

When Texas politicians swapped 3 million acres of Panhandle land to finance construction of a new capitol, the civilization of the Plains was assured. That land became the famous XIT ranch, surely the largest ever assembled. It spread over ten counties and extended for more than 200 miles from top to bottom. So large that management was troublesome for the syndicate that owned the ranch, the XIT ultimately was split into half-a-dozen parts, each a complete cattle operation. Six thousand miles of barbed wire enclosed the XIT's 150,000 head of cattle.

75

Other large ranches were founded, the LS and LX and LIT, the latter with more than 200,000 acres. But even as late as the 1890s, few more than a thousand people lived in the 26 counties of the Texas Panhandle. There was only one town of any size and import, Tascosa, and its peak had been reached.

Tascosa was born with the beginning of ranch life and for a couple of decades was a rough frontier town. Its first saloons were floored with $10-apiece planks hauled in from Dodge City, Kansas. There was a cemetery named Boot Hill, shootouts between cowboys and badmen, and a red light district called Hogtown. Billy the Kid and Pat Garrett had engaged in a friendly pistol competition (Garrett won). Ranchhands from the big spreads shot up the town regularly.

All that remains of Tascosa today are the cemetery and courthouse. Barbed wire fenced the town from its lucrative wagon train trade. After the railroad bypassed Tascosa, a new town, Amarillo, became the center of the Panhandle.

The XIT land always was intended to be sold to new settlers. Ranching, however profitable, was temporary. Those who came to settle on the Plains huddled like troglodytes in their prairie dugouts, prisoners in a country that punished them with heat and dust, took everything and returned little.

It was a land with temperature extremes ranging from 120 degrees to 23 degrees below, with hailstorms and duststorms and rainstorms, often all at once, and fierce thunder and lightning and tornadoes. And wind that never stopped riffling the prairie grasses. In winter the wind became a "norther," a sudden sweep of intense cold as soul biting as the *buran* of Siberia.

The wind, though, was the salvation of the High

Left– DALLAS SKYLINE AT NIGHT
Below– DALLAS CITY HALL
Overleaf– WEST END OF DALLAS SKYLINE

DALLAS SKYLINE WITH REFLECTIONS

Plains. It turned windmills which pumped water and, as early settlers discovered, that dark red earth was rich and would grow almost anything, if watered.

Today the Plains and Panhandle region of Texas is little more than one giant flat garden of wheat and oats and cotton, all irrigated from an underground pool of water that experts say will be depleted in this century.

The richness of West Texas's irrigated soils sped settlement, but rushes of people did not come until oil was struck, in Ranger and Borger and hundreds of other sites. West Texas was as oil-wealthy as East Texas.

West Texas remains a distant, formidable place of wonder. Towns and people have only given the appearance of subdued gentleness; the land still is harsh and rude, still is a region where, as one early settler complained, "Everything stings, sticks or stinks." West Texans, despite the clackety pumping of oil and water wells, re-

main dependent on the whims of weather, the cyclic moods of nature.

Those who live in Amarillo and Lubbock, largest of the Panhandle cities, have created a splendid life for themselves. Each city claims the title of the Panhandle's economic and social center. Perhaps both are. Amarillo's population is near 150,000, Lubbock's slightly over 200,-000. Each has colleges and museums and theaters and each, physically, is much like the other, because both were born from the surrounding flatness of the prairie.

Early settlers around Lubbock complained of prairie fires, sandstorms, blowing snow in winter, heat in summer, and droughts. Still the city was born and grew as the Panhandle turned itself into an irrigated farming empire and oil-producing region.

Today the streets are broad and straight, life seemingly pleasant in a city where the residents purposefully

FORT WORTH SKYLINE

planted 80,000 chrysanthemum blooms to give a bright color and lingering fragrance to their town.

Lubbock has the only state park in Texas located inside city limits. Mackenzie State Park was established to protect prairie dogs, and the colony attracts more visitors annually than any other state park. Once the prairie dogs numbered in the millions and their "towns" spread for miles across the Panhandle.

Amarillo appears larger than Lubbock but that is only because the land around it is even flatter than that surrounding Lubbock. Amarillo, too, bases its economy on oil, cattle, and farming.

Vast grain sorghum fields ring the city and that product feeds the cattle of the Panhandle, proving once again that those in the Texas Panhandle must provide for their own. Self-sufficiency is important because, as Amarillo residents are quick to point out, they live closer to

the capitals of three other states—New Mexico, Colorado, and Oklahoma—than Texas's capital, Austin.

However separated physically from the rest of Texas, the people of the Panhandle are addicted to their country, for there is a time in early spring when a softness comes to the plains and mountains, and tall buffalo grasses turn golden, as in Spanish Andalusia. There are fresh clovers on the pampas flatness, and riverlets run clear, and the epic grandness spreads over the horizon.

The marching flower army of Texas takes a long time to reach the Panhandle, but in late May or early June the highway north of Amarillo, through Dumas to Dalhart and Texline, is bordered by bluebonnets.

Wild verbena and Indian paint brush and sweet williams grow in the pastures, and Indian blanket and Queen Anne's lace and foxglove stray all the way across the flatness and beyond, into America.

Above– PRAIRIE GRASSES AT RIM
Below– ERODED MUDSTONES
and Right– LIGHTHOUSE ROCK IN PALO DURO CANYON STATE PARK

Left– RAIL LINE AND ELEVATORS, HAPPY
Above– LONE WINDMILL, TULIA
Below– COTTON, PANHANDLE

CITY of HISTORY, RIVER of GRACE

WHERE THE SAN ANTONIO AND GUADA-LUPE RIVERS MERGE IS NOT AN IMPORTANT TEXAS LANDMARK. AT THEIR CONFLUENCE TWO MILES NORTH OF TIVOLI, A TWO-CAFE VILLAGE ON THE COASTAL plain, the San Antonio is only a pipeline for the larger, more scenic Guadalupe, and its credentials as an essential river are uncertain.

Eastward the newly blended river pokes along for ten miles to enter the Gulf of Mexico at San Antonio Bay, where it pushes a cocoa stain into the blue sea.

The San Antonio is absorbed into the Guadalupe with no evidence of its phlegmatical grace, its episodic history. The stream, in its placid manner, is a Mississippi, a Yangtze, a Nile, and this rag of a river has been fought over, died beside, bled in, blessed, dammed, damned, and doomed.

Sonnets and songs celebrate its epic life. Poet pens acclaim its wandering way. Short stories and novels document its dramatic core. Men have set out for wars from the San Antonio and have come home to it from battles, too often in caskets. It has given love to presidents, shown God to priests. No other unnavigable American river floods across history with the adventuristic style of the San Antonio.

Sidney Lanier, the Georgia poet, once remembered his time with the river, when "memories came whispering down the current."

I understand his emotion for the river but cannot separate the river San Antonio from the city San Antonio, for the two have been one for almost 300 years. They are a single element, fused by time and circumstance. The river is the city's soul, as the Spanish population is its heart and the theatrical history its body. These three inseparable factors are almost seamless in their influence on the city, a gossamer coverlet for the social, cultural, and economic infrastructure that has become modern San Antonio.

The river is best seen from atop the Tower of the Americas, a 750-foot-tall concrete column rising out of HemisFair Plaza, the remaining park of HemisFair '68, the first and only world's fair with a pun in its name. Viewed from the tower's observation deck, the river below is like a lariat thrown carelessly on the ground, with coils and loops and curls, wandering everywhere and nowhere at once. In a mile-long run through the business district the river is crossed by 13 bridges yet has gone no more than 700 straight-line yards.

You cannot escape the river. Cross a bridge, round a corner and there it is again. Because of its river, believed Lanier, San Antonio is "a rare porcupine." Another kind of poet, the star-crossed blues singer, Jimmie Rodgers, said the river calmed his "gypsyfootin'," his "restless heels, soaring wings." Rodgers, the singing brakeman, came to San Antonio in 1924 with a single silver dollar and an ominous cough and until his death never left the city or the river for very long.

John Gunther believed that the city, with its river, was the equal of San Francisco, New Orleans, or Boston as a unique experience, but most outsiders still are startled to find a San Antonio in Texas.

The truth is, it is the state's most comfortable, functional city. If you're rich you make your money in less sensitive markets, like Houston or Dallas or Fort Worth, and you lavish it on San Antonio, and the river.

The annual army of marching flowers arrives in San Antonio at the first thought of March to create a bravura of blossoming days. Endemic within the city's spring are pink crepe myrtle, yellow retemas, beds of red cannas, and the white of magnolia. The Mexican colors of red and green dominate, and families move into the parks or walk beside the river.

Downtown, within one of its coils, the river winds through the city at a level 20 feet below the streets, a piece of outdoor sculpture formed with flagstoned walks and exotic plantings. A city park: *Paseo del Rio*, the river walk. One spring evening I stepped into the park and strolled the walks, which are lined with cottonwood, bald cypress, willows, wild olive, and palms, and scented by oriental jasmine and new roses and purple sage. The river was busy. A wedding party filled a passing barge, and a water taxi—a *chalupa*—went skimming by. Paddleboats thrashed the water. I sat for a long time near the Commerce Street Bridge, reflecting on the history of that unmagnificent span.

That is where the conquistadores arrived. They came

from the south, from across the Rio Grande and the virtually waterless, brushy *brasada.* The San Antonio River held sweet water for the Spanish explorers, who founded the city as the cynosure of a frontier of outpost missions stretching from what would become western Louisiana to Santa Fe.

Later, priests would wade the river at the Commerce Street point, going to their new mission, San Antonio de Valero, known today as the Alamo. Legend has it that the familiar name came from a regiment of Mexican soldiers who were quartered there so long, 11 years, that they began calling themselves *los alamos,* after the cottonwoods growing along the riverbanks. In 1736 a temporary footbridge—six large beams—was laid but ultimately removed because the wooden span became a handy access route for attacking Indians. By 1836 a plain yet strategically important footbridge had been built, and the city's defenders retreated across it to the Alamo and martyrdom. After the fort's fall, Santa Anna traversed the bridge to inspect his victory.

Over the years many notable visitors have written of the charm, the mystique of the Commerce Street Bridge. Frederick Law Olmsted, creator of New York City's Central Park, walked the bridge in the 1850s, writing later that the river flowed "rapidly but noiselessly." Lanier, by 1872 consumptive and dying, stood on the bridge and described "the green translucent stream flowing beneath." O. Henry, in his story, "A Fog in San Antone," wrote of his tubercular victim on a "little iron bridge . . . under which the small tortuous river flows." And it probably was the Commerce Street Bridge from which author Stephen Crane once leaped to save a drowning child.

In San Antonio, everyone comes to the river. A young Army lieutenant named Ike and his sweetheart, Mamie, held hands as they walked the riverbanks, bound for a Mexican dinner at the Original Cafe.

Another Army officer, Douglas MacArthur, came there regularly, as did a newly commissioned flier named Lindbergh; a mustached Teddy Roosevelt and, years later, his cousin Franklin; a tank commander called Patton; that old carouser and whiskey drinker Ulysses S. Grant; and a sag-eyed, stoop-shouldered small man named Robert E. Lee.

Lyndon Johnson and Lady Bird married in a nearby Episcopal church—with license No. 105133—and afterwards strolled over the bridge and to the river.

Today the river loop, the park, is lined with shops, good restaurants, and night clubs and is the center of all that occurs in San Antonio, from outdoor art shows that may attract 250,000 people on a sunny spring afternoon, to Fiesta, a week-long celebration each April of parades and costume balls and more than a little Spanish pomp and circumstance to celebrate the city's Hispanic heart.

No American city is more Spanish than San Antonio —it has five Spanish missions, four Spanish plazas, more Spanish-speaking, Spanish-surnamed people than Veracruz, Puebla, or San Luis Potosi, Mexico. Several radio and television stations broadcast solely in Spanish. In Market Square, one of those ancient plazas, there are shops of herb doctors—the *curanderos*—where potions of ground deer horn—*cuerno de venado*—and concoc-tions of sunflower seeds and kidney weed and creosote bush may be purchased. The San Antonio Yellow Pages even has a listing for "midwifery."

The Spanish of course came first, but San Antonio always has been a gathering place and crossroads of early America. Ethnic legacies abound. St. Patrick's Day has been stretched into a week-long celebration on the river, more often than not with the water tinted shamrock green. Each Sunday, the Chinese Baptist Church conducts sermons in two languages—English and Mandarin. The 50-voice Beethoven Maennerchor has been singing classical German music for more than 100 years. There is an annual Greek festival and a Lebanese fair complete with San Antonio-born belly dancers. Each August, the Texas Folklife Festival, one of the state's largest annual events, brings together more than 30 ethnic groups for an orgy of foods and music.

San Antonio has been called an ethnic gumbo, although the basic spice always is Spanish. Two hundred years of community togetherness has intermingled ethnic origins to the extent that there are families named O'Brien whose forefathers lived in the Canary Islands, blond-haired teutonic Garzas, and a Gonzales clan with relatives in Glasgow.

All of these multi-national influences have been part of an adventurous history of no small measure. Still remembered is the sight of Sunday dudes and their ladies riding ostriches in the parks. And a classic battle staged between a lioness and Mexican fighting bull (the bull won). And the Buckhorn Saloon, where cowboys were permitted to ride their horses up to the bar. In about 1868, an unknown hero employed at Marnisch Baer's confectionery shop invented the ice cream soda (the claim is disputed, but I choose to believe San Antonio's version). San Antonio is the city that invented that most palpable of Texas soul foods—chili. And in San Antonio, O. Henry invented an enduring western character, the Cisco Kid.

San Antonio is an uncommon place.

Not surprisingly, San Antonio's early planners did not anticipate the automobile. Many streets follow paths of old water ditches—the *acequias*—which nourished the early mission families who clustered around the traditional village squares. The city's downtown streets would more fittingly accommodate oxcarts and horses, and today those Spanish plazas are best reached by foot. Although of all of San Antonio's ancient squares, Alamo Plaza is the least attractive today, a walking tour of the city should begin there because, truthfully, San Antonio —and modern Texas—begin at the Alamo.

The plaza has become a major thoroughfare for city traffic, and only after dark, when the automobiles have gone, does the magic of yesteryear return, recalling a time when the square was bustling with withered old women in black mantillas hawking boutonnieres and thin Mexican candies, German burghers seeking a favorite beer garden, and intemperate cowboys firing off their pistols for the pure hell of it.

Facing Alamo Plaza the Menger Hotel still stands as it has for more than 120 years. In a corner of the lobby, before a giant fireplace, William Sidney Porter scratched short stories on long yellow pads. Only after he left San Antonio, having served a jail term for embezzling $554.48 from an Austin bank, did he become famous as O. Henry, remembering the city in seven of his stories, and Texas in two dozen others.

Oscar Wilde, dressed in yellow silk waistcoat, blue tie, green cape, and black breeches, fed raw meat to alligators living in a patio pool at the Menger. Cattlemen, those prairie Caesars of Texas, headquartered in the Menger. Richard King, owner of the sprawling King Ranch, often rode the 20 miles from his house to the ranch's front gate, then boarded a stagecoach to San Antonio to meet his friend, Shanghai Pierce, another cattleman, at the Menger.

The hotel's European-trained kitchen staff brought forth specialties like *Grouse Farci aux Truffes* and *Cailles en Aspic,* and from the wine cellar, *Duc de Reichstadt* champagne. King and Pierce, though, preferred more local fare such as buffalo hump roast, wild turkey, deer loin—and turtle steak fresh from the San Antonio River.

Lee and Grant, FDR, generals Patton, Pershing, Zachary Taylor, and William Tecumseh Sherman, writers Bret Harte and Joaquin Miller, capitalist Jay Gould, frontiersmen Buffalo Bill Cody and Sam Houston, actresses Anna Held and Sarah Bernhardt—all trod the marble-floored lobby during the Menger's halcyon years.

Teddy Roosevelt stopped at the Menger when he arrived in San Antonio to form his Rough Riders—the First U.S. Volunteer Cavalry of the Spanish-American War. Mostly they were young San Antonians, but West Texas cowboys signed up, too, men with strange names like "Sore-eyed Bill" and "Shirt-collar Sam." There were others, such as William Tiffany of the Fifth Avenue Tiffanys and Hamilton Fish, Jr., termed a "millionaire playboy," who lined up at the Menger's bar—still in use today—to become Rough Riders. Each had to swear he was "entirely sober when enlisted."

Next door to the Menger is the Alamo, Texas's best-known shrine. Trouble had been brewing for over a year when 187 men died there in 1836, at the hands of Santa Anna and his vast army. By 1835, the desire of some Texans for independence from Mexico had led to armed revolt and a series of military confrontations. On December 9, Texas rebels took San Antonio from the Mexican forces garrisoned there. It was to put down these insurgents that dictator Antonio Lopez de Santa Anna marched his armies north across the Rio Grande.

The 104 men who were left to defend San Antonio knew that they faced nearly insurmountable odds. As they withdrew to fight from behind the walls of the Alamo, William Travis, co-commander with James Bowie, issued a plea for aid "with all dispatch." Sam Houston, who was engaged with Mexican troops near Goliad, 100 miles away, sent 30 men, all he could spare. Soon they were joined by a small band of reinforcements led by Tennessean Davy Crockett. Thirty more slipped through enemy lines from Gonzales.

The heroes came from varied backgrounds. Only a handful were native Texans. Most were adventurers from the United States who shared the Texans' desire for self-government. Thirty-six were English and the others in-

DOWNTOWN SAN ANTONIO RIVER SCENE

cluded Scots, Irish, two Germans, and a Dane. Only six had been in Texas for as long as five months. Few were literate. It is unlikely that more than half of them could have read the Texas Declaration of Independence which was adopted, unbeknownst to them, at the Constitutional Convention four days before their defeat on March 6.

Historian Seyers believed that until the last the men never really thought they would die there. Travis was not, Seyers wrote, "oriented toward martyrism."

But Travis's message to the people of Texas, containing the words, "I am besieged. . . . I shall never surrender or retreat," is one of the great documents of courage in history.

The men died fighting inside the stone and adobe walls. Santa Anna, who considered himself the equal of Napoleon, prolonged the final attack with bittersweet tactics. He alternately had marksmen fire on the Texans, then followed with classical music played by his regimental band. Santa Anna's strength was in masses of men, and on the 13th day of siege, when he raised the red flag of no quarter and commanded his trumpeters to sound the chilling *deguello,* 2,000 Mexican soldiers swarmed over the Alamo's walls, and a legend was born.

"Remember the Alamo!" first was heard little more than a month later, when Sam Houston's soldiers, seeking to avenge the martyrs and win independence, surprised and overran Santa Anna's army at San Jacinto. In 1849, the first U.S. Army garrison arrived in San Antonio to restore the Alamo. Today the city is headquarters of the Fourth U.S. Army and houses large numbers of military personnel at Fort Sam Houston, Randolph Field, Kelly Field, and Lackland Air Force Base, also a medical center of renown.

Military Plaza, across the river, is less special historically than Alamo Plaza but more typical of San Antonio. It was a military compound as early as 1731 and later an outdoor market where citizens bargained for vegetables, hens for Sunday dinners, fiery bowls of chili, mockingbirds in wicker cages, buffalo hides, and donkeys. Some people also had teeth pulled alfresco by itinerant dentists; others had their pockets picked; some were shot by cowboys or hanged by vigilantes.

A magnificent oak once stood at the plaza's southeast corner. It was called the "Law of Mondragon," named for a vigilante leader. It was a hanging tree, about which was composed a ballad containing these words:

> The Law of Mondragon
> All Texans will endorse
> That here in San Antone
> You must not steal a horse.

The last vestige of Military Plaza's past is in the Spanish Governors' Palace. Neither a palace nor occupied by governors, it was the residence of the ranking emissary of the King of Spain. The mustard-colored structure is the last remaining example in Texas of an aristocratic Spanish house. Fully restored, the low-profiled home was built in 1749. It is furnished with period artifacts, including carved canopy beds covered by gold damask cloth and tooled leather chairs in the *sala*—a room for entertaining.

Main Plaza—*Plaza Principal de Bexar*—should be

seen at dawn. In the civil twilight of a spring morning, the sounds of the bells of San Fernando Cathedral fill the square, along with the smells of coffee and frying bacon, and the special aroma of tortillas from nearby cafes.

San Fernando Cathedral has stood in the plaza for two and a half centuries. On exceptionally clear mornings sunlight forms an aureole above the cathedral's bell towers, each of which is crowned by a white cross.

To see the reflected halo you must stand on the steps of a Gothic redstone courthouse south of the church. There is only a brief moment when the effulgence of light sprays the towers, but it is a remarkable sight and one that has been repeated for centuries, during which a lengthy melodrama of history has played below.

In 1749, Apaches came to settle a peace with Spain. The treaty—soon broken—was consummated in the plaza with the ritualistic burial of a live horse, a tomahawk, a lance, and six arrows. Those peace tokens still are there, now under the grounds of a small green park. In front of San Fernando in 1813, the American Volunteers made North America's first declaration of independence from Spain. Years later, Davy Crockett stood on a wooden box in this square to speak in his backwoodsy, mesmeric style to men who were destined to die at the Alamo. In a hotel across the plaza, a troubled Robert E. Lee paced away the night agonizing over personal loyalties. By sunrise on that day in 1861, he had decided to join the Confederacy.

Not within walking distance of downtown but still beside the river are San Antonio's Spanish missions: San Juan Capistrano, Concepcion, San Francisco de la Espada, and San Jose, a natural historic site and a magnificent architectural psalm in stone and mortar.

Many different events led to the creation of San Antonio, a city in the path of history and time and geography. But today, realistically, the river cannot live except by municipal support, much as civic patrons support an opera company or a symphony orchestra.

San Antonio is located on the southern edge of the Edwards Plateau and a geological aberration, the Balcones Fault, a series of underground vaults created by slippage of rock strata. Rainwater flows from Edwards Plateau into the limestone vaults. North of San Antonio this water flow is shaped much like a candelabra, its upraised arms representing tributaries, and the San Antonio River, the spine. Once the river flowed from a gushing spring, and the spring water flooded the river throughout its 180-mile run to the Gulf of Mexico. But the springs long ago were siphoned from their limestone caverns for industrial and residential use.

Today the San Antonio River Authority controls the river's use and fixes its rate of flow, pumping 879,000,000 gallons of well water annually into the streambed from a large brown pipe in Brackenridge Park, the city's central green space.

Regardless of its source, the San Antonio remains a nurturing parent, though the civilization it has nourished is perhaps not one ranking with that of the Euphrates or the Brahmaputra. It is a thin stream, shallow and unpretentious, yet there is in its pure, milky green water a charismatic splendor no one ever can adequately explain.

WEST of the PECOS

YOU COME OUT OF THE HEAT AND DUST AND LONELINESS OF NEW MEXICO'S SOUTHERN DESERT TO A FLAT PLACE BEARDED WITH CREOSOTE BUSH AND PITTED BY SURFACE MINES, A PLACE WHERE 25 ACRES WILL NOT FEED A POOR cow. Along U.S. 180 out in the far western arm of Texas are tiny towns, filling station and rusty trailerhouse towns, and the morose clacking of hammerhead oil pumps sucking up their 40 barrels a day from the earth. It is a country of terse finality in shape and tone and mood.

Below White City, where tourists turn toward Carlsbad Caverns, the highway sags below the horizon, then begins to climb. The road's path rises and it is almost as though the land is a ramp leaning against the base of El Capitan.

And then the road reaches Nickel Creek Station, one of those two-gas-pump towns, and the Guadalupe Mountains are behind: El Capitan's 1,000-foot-long, sad, white face; Guadalupe Peak, Texas's highest point; and its neighbors, Pine Top and Bush mountains, Shumard and Bartlett peaks.

Composed of limestone, the Guadalupes are an ocean reef raised from a Permian sea 200 million years ago. No other landlocked reef in the world is as well circumscribed and sustained, and fossils from the sea can be uncovered on the very peaks of the mountains.

From the ship's-prow boldness of El Capitan and northward for 77,000 acres, much of the mountains' area in Texas has become Guadalupe Mountains National Park, one of America's most remote and least-visited preserves.

Geologically and biologically the park is unique and beyond duplication, especially within the thin confines of McKittrick Canyon, behind Pine Top, with a balance of nature so delicate environmentalists fear that even the most limited access of man will unsettle what it has taken more than 10,000 years to produce.

Men were there 12,000 years ago. They are little in evidence and presence today. The Apaches hid within the Guadalupes; prospectors found gold there; and other, milder men felt the mountains' beauty "proved God."

We went up the mountain at dawn as the sun burned away the haze on Pine Top. The trail to the gorge through which we rode and would climb was level and flanked by agave and sotol. The trail up the canyon was narrow, rocky. With hand tools and courage, Mexican laborers cut the tight path decades ago. The horses we rode were called "rock horses" because they were experienced on the trail, but still their hooves slipped on the loose gravel and skidded over the stones.

The canyon trail rises up in cutbacks almost 4,000 feet. A dozen times it crosses a dry streambed, sneaks behind the monster boulders that have fallen from the mountain, and climbs over rock ledges for which we dismounted and led the horses.

To the left is Guadalupe Peak, a mountain of little distant beauty. That it is Texas's highest point—8,751 feet—is the mountain's only distinction from afar. Behind us stood the rock face of El Capitan, which can be seen from 80 miles into the surrounding flatness. Its great oyster-colored face, often mistaken for Guadalupe, has for centuries been a guiding reference point—for Spanish conquistadores, for Apaches who held the mountains sacred, for men in covered wagons heading West, for the Butterfield stagecoaches which passed beneath, for troops of U.S. Cavalry who served nearby.

Above the canyon the path to Pine Top becomes loosely packed gravel and sharp turns. You must ride 300 feet to rise vertically by 50 feet. The horses slip in the gravel, which slides down the sharp mountainside. A horse falls to its knees, its rear legs hanging over the point of the trail. The rider jumps off but the horse struggles to its feet, rears, and falls on him. His head strikes a rock and he is cut on each forearm by the stones but he is safe, only bruised and dazed. Someone says, after the injured rider remounts, that the trail seems dangerous, in need of repair, and the guide nods agreement and moves again upward.

The trail topped out and we rode into the bowl, a depression in which a conifer forest grows and has thrived for thousands of years. The forest is thick in the basin. Fir, Ponderosa pine, oak, the red-skinned Texas madrone, a beautiful tree, and stands of maple, cause slow riding.

We ate lunch in a pine draw, out of the wind, and later rode to the mountain's southern edge. U.S. 180 can be seen from the mountain, a line of gray across the desert, heading west through the salt marshes to El Paso.

The horizon is pale and dusty, and the grasses far below are a poorly defined green film, like the algae clouding a muddy pond.

Wreckage of a light plane lies on the side of a mountain across from us, in full sight of the highway and civilization. Yet searchers could not find the plane for 31 days after it crashed, sometime back in the 1950s.

Guadalupe is more distinctively shaped than Pine Top and assumes a stance of grandeur. Atop Guadalupe, at the precise measured highest point of Texas, is a five-foot-high metal pyramid placed decades ago by American Airlines as a monument to its pioneer pilots who once flew their old Ford tri-motor planes over the mountains toward Los Angeles.

Airlines were much more loosely defined and informal then and pilots, mostly Texans, often performed little favors for other Texans who chose to live out there in the wastelands. Once a week, a plane would detour south from Guadalupe and pass over a ranchhouse. The pilot would fly low and dump a sack of mail and newspapers to the rancher who lived a mere 40 miles from the nearest road, 60 miles from the closest town. Distance is a mean reality of western Texas.

The scene from Pine Top is a sobering one, and I know of a visitor there who once looked upon the surrounding mountains, on the desert below, and apologized to God for intruding on the silence.

There are elk there. We saw their droppings on Pine Top. Wild turkeys and black bear, mountain lions and deer live in remote canyons; razorback hogs, released years ago by a rancher in southern New Mexico, have found sanctity within the Guadalupes. In McKittrick Canyon, a place of rare, precious beauty, the narrow, clear, spring-fed creek is home to Texas's only trout.

McKittrick is a relic, a living antiquity. The creek is lined with juniper, the madrone, gray oak, fir and maple, the latter a remnant of what once was a great forest of the trees. There is a variety of honeysuckle in McKittrick that is not known to grow anywhere else on earth.

One can walk into McKittrick on a trail that follows the small creek for almost three miles before it blunts into a rock ledge that forms a small waterfall. At one point the southern wall of McKittrick rises almost 2,000 feet to the rear bluffs of Pine Top, and below that escarpment the stream forms shallow pools like shiny beads in which trout swish over smooth rocks.

Once Apaches—the Mescaleros—lived within the canyon, within the mountains. The Spanish found them there. The Guadalupes were a sacred sanctuary for them, a home for the mythical gods of the sun and moon, and, according to legend, a storehouse for their gold.

Geologists will tell you gold does not appear in reef formations like the Guadalupes, but the Apaches and a man called Old Ben Sublett would have argued the scientific fact.

Old Ben lived 150 miles east, in Odessa, then, in the 1870s and 1880s, a rude frontier town of the desert. Sublett, history insists, was a barfly and failure until an old Apache told him of gold in the Guadalupes, gold only the Indians could find.

Sublett disappeared into the desert, marching west to the mountains, and when he returned he had nuggets of gold. For two decades the old man made trips to the mountains and returned with gold and, though followed by others, no one ever knew his source.

Once he took his son with him to the cache and the boy, then scarcely 13, later in life vaguely remembered a ravine and a cave, but not the trail. Old Ben died in 1892 without revealing the site of his Apache gold, and his son searched for it in vain until his death in the 1950s.

There was gold, but was it from a natural mine? Or was it gold the Apaches stole from others and secreted in their sacred mountains?

The Apaches, North America's best guerrilla fighters, used the mountains as an ambush point for passing wagon trains and stagecoaches. The Butterfield Overland Mail Line, established in 1858 to carry mail and passengers from St. Louis to San Francisco, passed just west of Guadalupe Peak.

After the Civil War soldiers entered the vast triangle of Far West Texas to do battle with the Apaches, to clear the way for westward-advancing settlers. One of the largest military posts was south, in the Davis Mountains, lodged in the formidable Limpia Canyon.

Fort Davis, even today as a restored national historic site, looks the way a real western fort should. It housed black cavalry troops whom the Indians called "buffalo soldiers," both as a name of identification and respect.

The officers of Fort Davis were white, and there is a legend about one of the officers and an Indian girl that is still recounted in the shadows of the Guadalupes.

Indian Emily, the story says, was a pretty Apache girl wounded in a raid and restored to health by the mother of a young lieutenant, Tom Easton. Following her recovery, she remained at the fort as a maid for the white woman, and secretly fell in love with the lieutenant.

Tom Easton announced his engagement to Mary Nelson, daughter of another officer at the fort, and Indian Emily left. She was not seen for a year and the Eastons presumed she had returned to her tribe.

Late one night a fort sentry saw a figure coming out of the canyon's blackness. He cried, "Halt!", but the figure came straight toward him. He fired. It was Indian Emily. Critically wounded, she told of a pending dawn attack by Apaches. In the best tradition of all such Hollywoodish legends, the fort, and Tom Easton, were saved. Indian Emily died. A monument beside U.S. 180, beneath the Guadalupes, testifies to Emily's bravery and her love for the white lieutenant.

Before we left Pine Top for the three-hour ride down the twisting, rocky trail, we rode back through the forest.

For an instant four deer, a huge buck, a pair of does, and a fawn, stood in a clearing. We watched through the trees. Then a horse snorted and the deer lifted their white flags and ran away into the deeper regions of the forested bowl. When the deer had gone, we rode out of the forest and down the mountain in the late afternoon sun.

The road to El Paso from the Guadalupes is long and straight and boringly flat. It is a highway built for speed, for the exigency of moving vehicles through the vastness of the desert.

Stagecoaches, four-horse Concords, once rushed through the searing desert toward El Paso with the same urgency, pausing only at waystations to change horses. One station was nestled under Guadalupe Peak. The next was at Hueco Tanks, now a state park, but once the only sure water supply between the Guadalupes and El Paso.

The tanks are natural reservoirs found in recesses of granite rocks, which catch and hold rainwater. They served everyone passing by—from Indians to goldhunters on their way to California, from outlaws with rustled cattle to weary stagecoach travelers.

Water and another natural element, salt, both were necessities for travelers going west. Salt Flat, today only a huddle of buildings off the highway near the Guadalupes, in 1877 was the site of the Salt War over ownership of the surface salt deposits all around.

The highway continues on through the flat, stern wilderness and finally, simply and suddenly, there is El Paso, an uncommonly far place out on the calloused finger of desert America calls the Southwest, spread before the final gray crags of the American Rockies, an autonomy of time and space. Settled amid the desert starkness, the city seems distant, seems a quasi-civilized frontier outpost, but that is an illusion. El Paso today is isolated by the mind's eye, nothing else.

Whenever I go to El Paso I drive up into the mountains above it, to the hip of Mount Franklin, below the mile-high notch called Smuggler's Gap, to sit and feel the history of the place. Looking south, Mexico is on the right, and left is Far West Texas.

There is El Paso below, and without interruption, Juarez, Mexico, two cities bound together by the cement furrow of the Rio Grande and by their seeming isolation. A million people, Americans and Mexicans, live there, sharing a culture and history that have been intertwined for three centuries. They are as one.

Beyond Juarez, across the dry river and south into the beige distance, is the path of the past.

Conquistadores came from the south, tracking the myths of the seven golden cities—"a galaxy of cities, the inhabitants of which wore civilized raiment, lived in palaces ornamental with sapphires and turquoises, and possessing gold without end," as Horgan has explained.

Eighty years before the Pilgrims landed at Plymouth Rock, soldiers of Francisco Vasquez de Coronado rode through El Paso del Norte—the Pass of the North—seeking the rich land of Cibola. Pedro de Castaneda, a diarist of the period, wrote that the Spanish never found their golden cities but, he reasoned with indisputable logic, they "found a place in which to search."

From that mountain overlook below Smuggler's Gap, the Rio Grande can be seen coursing southeast, following an irrigated valley green with truck crops. A field of vegetables there beside the river is probably the longest continuously farmed piece of land in North America. And off in the distance, a white rumpled interruption of the flat horizon, are the Spanish missions of Ysleta, Texas's oldest community. Once the village was in Mexico, but the river's course changed, leaving it in Texas. Founded as the mission Corpus Christi de la Isleta del Sur in 1681, the town at first was a refuge for Tigua Indians, who re-mained loyal to the Spanish during a general Indian uprising in New Mexico.

Through the centuries the Tiguas were absorbed into white civilization. By the early 1970s, when the federal government officially recognized them as an Indian tribe, fewer than 100 remained.

With official recognition, establishment of a reservation in El Paso, and the infusion of federal money, the Indians set about to preserve their heritage, constructing an Arts and Crafts Center and restoring important early buildings in the village. Open daily, the tribal center has become El Paso's most popular visitor attraction as younger members of the tribe learn arts and crafts from elders. Among the buildings being restored are Socorro Mission, the oldest continuously active parish church in America, and San Elizario Mission, the latter dating to 1598. Mission Nuestra Señora del Carmen, parts of which date to 1682, also is being restored. Land around it has been in cultivation for more than 400 years.

The missions already were ancient when Comanches and Apaches ruled, when the Yuma stages passed, when West Texans, with the help of Mexican vaqueros, were giving rise to every blessed thing we now honor as The West. That was the real West out there, and El Paso, first known to Texans as Magoffinville—not a name to inspire poetry—was part of it.

El Paso was for centuries alone in that distant nook of Texas, and now its character is neither Texan nor Mexican, nor even New Mexican, which is a part of the ruling triumvirate, but something else, some special hybrid world. El Pasoans are an amalgam of all those influences.

Because the city emits an emotional essence, it is a town to walk in, to get close to.

San Jacinto Plaza, an ancient mid-city square, is a centerpiece of the past. Once camels from Smyrna, characters of that ignoble experiment in the desert by the U.S. Army, huddled in the plaza, and there was a pool of alligators, and Sunday band concerts were held.

Nearby the Jackass Mail stages paused, and a block farther on, four men died in five seconds of gunfire. A few steps beyond that, John Wesley Hardin, killer of 26 men, expired on the floor of the Acme Saloon, victim of a constable's bullet.

Often I stroll into Hotel Paso del Norte, which dates from the last century, and stare up at the delicate dome of Tiffany glass high above the lobby.

An effete touch decidedly out of place in macho El Paso, but no more anachronistic than the international trolley that once operated outside on San Antonio Street. From 1881 and for almost a century the streetcars passed back and forth over the Rio Grande to connect El Paso and Juarez, a transportation facility that proved the ease of moving between the two countries. The world's only international trolley, it ceased operations in the 1970s, the victim of fiscal difficulties.

Today's El Paso still does not have a skyline reflective of its large population. There are a few tall buildings, but they are dwarfed by the mile-high Franklin Mountains whose flanks rise out of the city. El Paso is wrapped around those mountains and is more compact than most desert communities.

Much is squeezed into the pass—Fort Bliss, a major U.S. military installation; a fine new multi-million dollar Civic Center; a zoo; and the campus of the University of Texas at El Paso.

As it does all of that far piece of Texas, the desert intrudes on modern El Paso, and the clear air, sunshine, and high altitude combine to make the city a popular retirement center.

"We have more sunshine than Mars," an El Pasoan once told me with typical Texas modesty, and that may be a true statement. Going into the 1980s the sun had been hidden behind clouds fewer than three dozen days in the previous 13 years.

It is best to remember that except for a few scattered settlements, Far West Texas was largely uninhabited until well into the 1920s. As late as 1931 there were fewer than 50 paved miles of highway between the upper Panhandle and Del Rio beside the Rio Grande. Many remote ranches and smaller villages did not receive electric service until the early 1950s.

Distance was the barrier to West Texas settlement. Distance, and the desert, the heat, the general lack of water, and the loneliness.

I remember an old cowboy telling me of a ranch on which he had worked in about 1900. The most distant pasture was 65 miles from the ranchhouse, and he often lived and worked away from headquarters five and six months at a time.

Even in my youth out there it was nothing to drive 80 miles to see a movie or buy a beer.

Far West Texas was an inhospitable place, especially before the innovations of air-conditioning and superhighways. A verse in an old prairie song told the story: "The heat in the summer's a hundred and ten/Too hot for the devil and too hot for men."

Those first pioneers were prisoners in a great dusty prairied country that could not be gentled, and not everyone who came remained. For lack of building materials and to escape the heat, many families lived in dugouts. A cowboy once encountered a deserted dugout with this note attached to the front door:

> 20 miles to water
> 10 miles to wood
> 6 inches to Hell
>
> Gone back East to wife's family,
> make yourself to home.

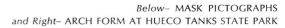

Below– MASK PICTOGRAPHS
and Right– ARCH FORM AT HUECO TANKS STATE PARK

For all of West Texas's unsociable ways, men came, lured by oil, and the region began filling up. Last to be occupied was Texas's ventricose belly, the Big Bend, here the physiognomy is one of wilderness, of distance and space, of colors washed and muted.

It can be argued that the Big Bend still has not been settled, especially around the national park, which is a mere three quarters of a million acres at the bottom of the bulge of the Rio Grande.

From San Antonio, it is 410 miles to park headquarters at Panther Junction, about the distance from Washington, D.C., to Boston. El Paso is 323 miles away. The nearest town of any size is Marathon, 70 miles distant, which has fewer than a thousand residents.

The Big Bend has always been an impregnable stone fortress that frustrated any real sense of civilization. "The tide of Spanish exploration split upon the rock formed by the Big Bend country and ebbed and flowed along either side," Horgan wrote.

However it is approached, the Big Bend is a thousand square miles of awesomeness. There is dignity and grandeur and a sort of controlled isolation. In winter months there is a grayness, a blandness that only emphasizes the vastness. The grasses are bleached white by the biological process of cool weather, and oaks and cottonwoods and cypress release their golden leaves.

Perhaps it is the clouds of winter. We rented horses in Chisos Basin, and rode up into the clouds on one of those wet, dingy days. Mount Emory wore a neckpiece of beige fog. Carter Peak, a needle-topped mountain, was an illusion behind the clouds.

The Window, an opening on the western side of the escarpment surrounding the basin, is washed by the valley's water between two rock cliffs. On clear days, you can see 80 miles into the Chihuahuan Desert from this spot. As we rode, the horses snorted and clopped and, like all gentle animals, wanted more to return to the corral than to walk in the clouds.

Through the Window, the desert was sunny in the late afternoon. Sunset was a brief flash of light between the wine-colored horizon and low clouds.

In the grayness of twilight we returned to the basin. That night it was cold and the clouds vanished. Casa Grande and Mount Emory, with cliffs of granite and volcanic residue, emerged above. The Chisos Basin, with or without clouds, is a spectacular centerpiece for Big Bend.

All around, the Chisos—the Ghost Mountains—form a mile-high spectacle above the desert. From the basin's South Rim, reached by horseback or hiking trail only, you can see the Rio Grande and Mexico's mountains, the Sierra del Carmen, with white cliffs and dark purple coloring, and Santa Elena Canyon, one of three massive gorges cut by the river.

It is not a gentle country—"scabrous," writer Jon McConal labeled the Big Bend. Born of volcanic upheaval, the land is rocky, dry. Only in the highest reaches of the mountains do sparse forests grow—white oak and live oak, long leaf pine, Mexican piñon, juniper, spruce, and the Arizona cypress. There are black bears in the forests, and panthers and bobcats; red deer and flowers fill the meadows in early spring.

The Big Bend has a violent history. First, the volcanoes' eruptions, then dinosauric monsters, and finally, man—the Indians, Mexican bandits, ranchers and gold smugglers, cowboys and outlaws. Pancho Villa raided into the Big Bend. The great Comanche War Trail ran through Twin Mule Ear Peaks and beyond, to Mexico, where the Indians wintered and raided isolated haciendas as far south as Durango.

There was a silver mine somewhere in the Big Bend in which Mexican criminals were forced to work. Soldiers blindfolded the men and marched them through the mountains to the mine, said to be in a sheer rock cliff of the Chisos Basin. One day Comanches attacked, massacring the soldiers and mine workers. One miner escaped, but he was never able to relocate the mine; no one has ever found the mine again.

Big Bend is scattered with the remains of yesterday's life. A deserted ranchhouse. A cold fire started by a sheepherder. Terlingua, Shaftner, Study Butte—crumbling shacks of mining dreams.

In a shattered kind of way, desolate Terlingua still lives as a ghost town of some reputation. Each fall it is the site of an international chili cooking competition. One mine is sometimes open, sometimes closed. Cinnabar—mercuric sulfide—is the treasure of Terlingua. Howard Perry discovered the mercury veins, worked the mines, and returned to New York a rich man. Later, he came back to the Big Bend with a bride. She stayed one day, then went home.

"If you believe in socialism, an eight-hour day or bathin' on a regular basis, you have no business out here," the late Buck Newsome, a horse wrangler of the Big Bend, once told me.

The Big Bend still is best seen by horse or mule but paved roads touch near most major points. Entering from Marathon on U.S. 385, the desert gives way to the mountains. The Chaneys are on the east. Westward is Santiago Peak, named for a Chisos Indian chief killed by Apaches and buried at its foot.

Persimmon Gap in the Santiago Range, the trail along which the Comanches migrated, precedes Dagger Mountain, its stony trunk protected by a barricade of Spanish dagger plants, their points as sharp and deadly as bayonets. And finally there is Panther Pass, and the road winds into the basin past Grapevine Hills and a park fossil display.

Big Bend is a paleontological nirvana, a kind of marvelous outdoor mortuary for beasts of the past. There scientists found the skull of a 35-million-year-old primate, a missing link of the monkey family; skeletons of prehistoric horses, dogs, and camels; and teeth of an ancient rhinoceros.

The most startling find was the skeleton of a pterosaur—a pterodactyl, or winged reptile—with a wingspan of 51 feet, as long as a boxcar. The largest previously found pterosaur had a wingspan of only 25 feet.

From the basin, there are two roads to the river and the remote villages that are vital links to the chain of life in the Big Bend. Ruidosa is nothing more than a few mud huts. Candelaria has a general store and a jail, an iron cage on a rock pile. Rio Grande Village has a larger general store and a ranger station. Over the river is Boquillas, a burg of no particular distinction except that enterprising Mexicans have established a rowboat ferry for visitors. Once into Mexico there are donkeys for rent for the short ride into Boquillas, where there are two cantinas and a souvenir shop.

In remote Big Bend, Americans and Mexicans easily and regularly cross the river into one another's territory. Either dollars or pesos are accepted at all stores along the river, and U.S. Border Service officers care only about the wax smugglers, who come into the park for the towering candelaria plants, whose waxy sap is a prime ingredient for some chewing gums and auto polishes.

The park's western road runs to Presidio along the river, but first branches south to Santa Elena Canyon, most spectacular of the three major stone clefts dug by the Rio Grande.

Sloping to the river, the road enters a startling strip of greenery in the beige world of Big Bend. For several miles along the river, a deep-soiled wash laid down eons ago by the sea nurtures a profusion of salt cedars and cottonwoods and sunflowers. Once a speculator grew cotton and even built a gin there, but transportation costs made the venture unprofitable, and the land has reclaimed the old cotton fields.

Viewed from ten miles away, Santa Elena Canyon is a dark, purplish slit in sheer cliffs; the grandeur, the immensity of the gorge, is not evident until you reach its mouth and look up 2,000 feet to the canyon's crown.

Santa Elena is cut through Mesa de Anguila, an uplifted block of limestone pitted with shallow caves in which swallows and wrens nest. Rafting through Santa Elena and the other major canyons, Mariscal and Boquillas, has become the major sporting event of Big Bend. You enter the river at Lajitas, another tiny village. At that point the Rio Grande has been replenished with water from the Conchos River and the boats skim away on a swift current.

Once I was in a six-man rubber raft, approaching the canyon entrance at sunrise, when the willows and bamboo stands along the banks were still shadowed. There were a dozen white water riffs, none dangerous, before the raft was drawn into the darkness of the canyon.

Santa Elena is 18 miles long. Since the average raft travels three miles an hour, the trip need take no more than a day, but many camp within the canyon, dragging their boats onto sandy strips under overhangs of rock. For most of its length, the canyon's walls rise straight up to 1,500 feet and more, and the river often narrows to no more than three dozen feet in places where it surges between fallen boulders.

The most dangerous area encountered by rafters is the Rockslide, where boulders the size of small houses have broken away and fallen into the river. There, the water churns and falls, and most rafters portage around the slide, as we did.

Beyond the slide the river is mostly calm. Boats drift with the current in the stone slit of Santa Elena and voices echo within its walls, startling the swallows and wrens.

The river's exit from Santa Elena is as sudden as its entrance. Our raft glided out of the dark canyon into bright sunshine and we went ashore near Terlingua Creek.

I have never rafted Mariscal, but those who have claim it is a more peaceful canyon. Comanches crossed the river in Mariscal at a break in the rock and wax smugglers ford the Rio Grande there today.

Boquillas is a less attractive canyon, shorter, but calm, too, and beyond it are the lower canyons of the Rio Grande, which have become favored canoeing stretches along a 90-mile run of the river. The lower canyons have been called the most remote river area in America and there is a continuing campaign to turn the entire stretch into a section of Big Bend National Park.

Canoeists usually enter at La Linda, below Boquillas, and leave the river 90 miles later near Dryden, a speck of a town on U.S. 90. If anything, the river is more remote there than within the Big Bend. There are no settlements between the two points and the area is a favorite crossing for illegal aliens from Mexico.

In caves in the canyon walls, high above the river, archeologists have found evidence of the Basket Makers, a tribe of Indians who lived on the Rio Grande thousands of years before the Spanish arrived. Also known as the Desert Indians, they were overrun six centuries ago by other tribes.

Near the lower canyons, where Judge Roy Bean held court, is Langtry. It was Eagle Nest Springs in 1882 when Bean, immortalized in *The Law West of the Pecos,* crossed Pecos Canyon to set up a saloon, and became absolute law where there was none. In retrospect, his was a ludicrous kind of jurisprudence, comic opera prairie justice. Drunks chained to bears. Dead men fined for whatever Bean could salvage from their pockets. But he was effective out there in the harsh desert.

He renamed his saloon Jersey Lily and his town, Langtry, all for actress Lillie Langtry. And he promoted an international heavyweight boxing championship at a period when Texas banned public prizefights. Ruby Robert Fitzsimmons, an Australian, and Peter Maher, an Irishman, came to Langtry to fight, trailed closely by Texas Rangers armed with orders to arrest everyone, including Roy Bean. The judge moved everybody to a sandbank ring on the other side of the Rio Grande in Mexico, and the fight went off as scheduled. Judge Bean even sold beer at a dollar a glass.

The starkness of this withered segment of Southwest Texas is hypnotic, enticing; the grotesquely forbidding mountains, grandly majestic; and the funereal desert, a soothing narcotic. What appears to be is not. It is a land of survivors, and harsh beauty. Only the dark mysticism of Hispanics could decipher the Big Bend. An unknown Mexican vaquero long ago said of the place, "You go south from Fort Davis and after a while you come to the place where the rainbows wait for the rain, and the big river is kept in a stone box, and water runs uphill, and the mountains float in the air."

German artist Ludwig Bemelmans once sampled Far West Texas, its Big Bend, its desert barrenness, the vast grandeur, and afterwards said, "It is what Beethoven reached for in music. It will make you breathe deeply whenever you think of it, for you have inhaled eternity."

Right– FLOWERS AT DEVIL RIDGE NEAR VAN HORN
Overleaf– GYPSUM SAND DUNES, GUADALUPE MOUNTAINS

Left– EL CAPITAN FROM GUADALUPE PEAK
Below– EL CAPITAN AND GUADALUPE MOUNTAINS NATIONAL PARK

Left– CHOLLA IN DAVIS MOUNTAINS
Above– CENTURY PLANT IN BIG BEND NATIONAL PARK

Left– RIO GRANDE WEST OF REDFORD
Below– STRAWBERRY HEDGEHOG CACTUS AND RIO GRANDE

Below– RIO GRANDE IN SANTA ELENA CANYON
Right– RIO GRANDE AND BIG HILL OVERLOOK
Overleaf– RARE FROST STORM IN THE CHISOS MOUNTAINS

122

Left– DRY CASCADE IN LIMESTONE NEAR LANGTRY
Below– BUZZARDS, CHISOS MOUNTAINS